A Reason to Believe meets us in the upside-down world of moral relativism and scientific naturalism with lucid and reasonable answers. Dr. Elmarie Meintjes approaches some of the deepest questions of life with a scientific mind and a theistic worldview. This book will help you dig deeper into the challenges of our culture and strengthen your faith in the sufficiency of God's word. Mastery of these contents will surely prepare a generation of God's faithful servants to engage the world in which we live with a confident ability to display convincing reasons for belief. May you be blessed and may God be glorified with these wonderful pages!

- Richmond Goolsby
Director, North Texas Baptist Association,
Lewisville, TX

In today's incoherent and disjointed global culture, especially in our Western educational universe, innumerable students are daily fed a regimen of 'Reasons NOT to Believe' in a post-grave Life. This LIFE was guaranteed to those who BELIEVE, by the august and peerless God and Lord Jesus Christ, when 2 millennia ago, He burst forth from His tomb. To counter the noisily trumpeted evolutionary views, Dr. Elmarie Meintjes has published a profoundly simple, readable, yet thoroughly scientific text. May I highly recommend to all school administrators, science teachers and students that they include a copy of *A Reason To Believe* in their curriculum.

- Rev. Dale Cutlip
General Director, GlobeWorks International Ministries,
Birmingham, AL

I am thrilled to recommend this book to you! I could not put it down. Dr. Meintjes has written a well-researched, eloquent, easy-to-understand book, which puts the puzzle pieces of our life map together. *A Reason to Believe* provides tools for students to examine scientific claims with 'cordial skepticism.' At 103 pages, this thin paperback seems like a quick-read, but it is packed with questions and Bible studies that will enhance further understanding and facilitate hours of discussion. I highly recommend this book to supplement any science textbook and for any reader who desires to give an answer for 'a reason to believe.'

- Anita Nelson
Home-based Educator, TX

ELMARIE MEINTJES, DVM, M.S.

A REASON TO BELIEVE

TechnoNature Books
P.O. Box 238
Frisco, Texas 75034

Book cover design by Steve Miller, SteveMiller3D.com.

ISBN: 978-0-692-68582-2

For more information, please email: inquiries@technonature.com.

To my three precious sons

and all the sons and daughters on this planet.

Because it matters in heaven what you choose on earth.

CONTENTS

Why This Book?

"Helmuth feels his thoughts changing, charging ahead to a dangerous place. Slowly, an idea rises to the surface and floats in front of Helmuth. He catches it, breathes it in and it grips him. It won't let him go. He snaps on the light, takes out a piece of paper and jots down everything he can remember from the BBC broadcast. By midnight, he completed an essay titled, '*Who Is Lying?*'"[1]

Helmuth, a German teenager, could stay silent no longer. News from the small shortwave radio hidden in his room gripped his soul. News that Hitler would not allow the Germans to hear. He typed tirelessly through the nights and left his letters in strategic places. Helmuth dared to tell the truth, knowing it could cost him his life.

People eventually rebuilt broken lives and cities after the dreadful war. A new, liberated world emerged; a world of freedom and prosperity, wrapped in luxuries of modern technology. Most, however, are all too familiar with the cauldron of hopelessness, injustice, poverty, abuse and suffering that kept right on sputtering. Life is hard and difficult to understand, the truth like silly putty. With a moral compass resembling a fan, it seems impossible to find meaning and direction in the sea of life.

Ignoring a problem of this magnitude is not an option for most of us. One day, I watched some ants tackle a cookie. Instead of dragging the mammoth treasure, they deftly chopped off bite-size pieces and scurried off to their nest. We too can tackle the nebulous problem of life in bite-size pieces. Then, we can link the pieces like a puzzle, a "Life Puzzle," to build the big picture of meaning, purpose and direction.

Despite his youth, Helmuth already had the important puzzle pieces in place. Therefore, he could separate right from wrong, conquer his fears and act with conviction and purpose. In his upside-down world, Helmuth made a difference; his life had meaning that extended beyond this world. More importantly, on the day Helmuth faced his executioners, he was not lost in a storm of confusion and despair. He had a reason to believe in the living God who cares. Do you?

---

[1] S. C. Bartoletti, *The Boy Who Dared.* Scholastic Press, 2008, 121.

Chapter 1

The Life Puzzle

In a debate between Dr. Stephen Hawking, a professor of mathematics at Cambridge University, and Dr. John Lennox, a professor of mathematics at Oxford University, Dr. Hawking said, "Religion is a fairy story for people afraid of the dark." Dr. Lennox quickly retorted, "On the contrary! Atheism is a fairy story for people afraid of the light."[1]

These scientists have two opposite Life Puzzles, because they chose different pieces for their puzzles. In fact, many puzzles have crooked pieces jammed together; but the puzzle owners cannot, or will not, acknowledge it. As a result, you will find quite an assortment of Life Puzzles in this world. Below are a few you may recognize:

- The atheist puzzle is the universe and the particles it consists of. The puzzle is defined by scientists and limited to the physical world. It is void of purpose and anything spiritual or supernatural. Because the atheists' world is limited to the physical realm, they have to believe in the theory of evolution to explain their origin. They lack a puzzle piece for eternal destiny.

- Central to the Buddhist puzzle is the wheel of life, representing reincarnation. Buddhists meditate to achieve enlightenment, and perceive the world in some sense as unreal in order to be happier and more compassionate. They follow the teachings of Buddha, especially the four noble truths regarding suffering (the truth about suffering, the cause, the end and the path to the end of suffering). Their eternal destiny puzzle piece is a blissful nothingness called "nirvana." Buddhists also believe that devas, characters from other realms, do not play a role in our world.

- Allah, the creator of the universe as revealed through the Qur'an, is a corner piece to the Muslim puzzle. This group's puzzle includes pieces of eternal paradise, obedience to Allah and the command to perform jihads. The most literal reading of the Qur'an implies that by sacrificing your own life in the name of Allah, you earn assurance to reach paradise.[2]

- Most African tribes have a puzzle piece about a supreme being who made them. However, they also worship idols of gods like the sun and forefather spirits who

---

[1] J. Lennox, *Science and Faith,* 2013 Pensmore Dialogue.

[2] Sura 3:157 , <compellingtruth.org/assured-paradise.html>

require sacrifice, sometimes even the sacrifice of their children. Their eternal destiny pieces include "good spirit" or "bad spirit."

These puzzles are so radically different that they cannot possibly all be true! The French essayist, Michel de Montaigne, said it best in his essay, *Of Liars,* that there are a thousand ways to miss the bull's-eye, but only one way to hit it. Only one Life Puzzle can have pieces that match flawlessly.

This guide will take you on a remarkable journey of adding some of the most important pieces to your own Life Puzzle. Life actually becomes quite a ride when the pieces click into place, when you gain insight, clarity and an unshakable hope.

If all else fails, read the instructions for building your Life Puzzle:

- ✓ The corner pieces of this puzzle are *Truth, Science, Man* and *God.*
- ✓ Be critical. Verify information for yourself.
- ✓ Do not attempt to force-fit pieces together.
- ✓ The question sections have the most valuable puzzle pieces.
- ✓ Most questions contain references to Bible verses that you can find in the "Answers from the Bible" sections.

Your turn to dig deeper: The Life Puzzle

1. What does an atheist believe regarding a supreme being or beings?
    a. Were there atheists in King Solomon's time? (Read Psalm 14:1). You can find the scriptures referenced for each question in the "Answers from the Bible" below. Unless otherwise indicated, all scriptures are quoted from the New King James Version. Different Bible translations in many languages are available at <biblegateway.com>.
    b. Can you prove God does not exist?

2. What did God command His followers regarding worship? (Read Exodus 20:1-6 and Isaiah 42:8).

3. The Israelites repeatedly turned away from the one true God to worship demons and idols. (Read Deuteronomy 32:17).
    a. What were the consequences? (Read 2 Chronicles 24:18, Psalm 115:4-8).
    b. What happened to the god "Dagon?" (Read 1 Samuel 5:2-4).
    c. Did people in the New Testament worship idols? (Read Acts 17:22-23).
    d. Can you name a few religions that still require idol worship today?
    e. Do you have any idols? (Read Colossians 3:5).

4. In Genesis 22, God commanded Abraham to sacrifice his only son.
    a. What helped Abraham to be obedient? (Read Hebrews 11:17-19).
    b. What was the consequence of Abraham's obedience? (James 2:21-23).
    c. God did not let Abraham offer Isaac, what did He do instead? (Read Genesis 22:11-14).
    d. By not letting Abraham sacrifice Isaac, God also taught Abraham an important lesson about child sacrifice. Can you explain this? (Read Deuteronomy 12:31).
    e. Abortion is legal in many countries, but is it right? Is it different from sacrificing a child?

Answers from the Bible

1. **Psalm 14:1:** "The fool says in his heart, 'There is no God.' They are corrupt, they have done abominable works; there is no one who does good."

2. **Exodus 20:1-6:** "And God spoke all these words: 'I am the LORD your God, who brought you out of Egypt, out of the house of bondage. You shall have no other gods before Me. You shall not make for yourself a carved image – any likeness of anything that is in heaven above, or that is in the earth beneath, or that is in the water under the earth; you shall not bow down to them nor serve them. ...'"

   Isaiah 42:8: "I am the LORD, that is My name; and My glory I will not give to another, nor My praise to carved images."

3. **Deuteronomy 32:17:** "They sacrificed to demons, not to God, to gods they did not know, to new gods, new arrivals that your fathers did not fear."

3a. **2 Chronicles 24:18:** "Therefore, they left the house of the LORD God of their fathers, and served wooden images and idols; and wrath came upon Judah and Jerusalem because of their trespass."

Psalm 115:4-8: "Their idols are silver and gold, the work of men's hands. [5]They have mouths, but they do not speak; eyes they have, but they do not see; [6]They have ears, but they do not hear; noses they have, but they do not smell; [7]They have hands, but they do not handle; feet they have, but they do not walk; nor do they mutter through their throat. [8]Those who make them are like them; so is everyone who trusts in them."

3b. **1 Samuel 5:2-4:** "When the Philistines took the ark of God, they brought it into the house of Dagon and set it by Dagon. [3]And when the people of Ashdod arose early in the morning, there was Dagon, fallen on its face to the earth before the ark of the LORD. So, they took Dagon and set it in its place again. [4]And when they arose early the next morning, there was Dagon, fallen on its face to the ground before the ark of the LORD. The head of Dagon and both the palms of its hands were broken off on the threshold; only Dagon's torso was left of it."

3c. **Acts 17:22-23:** "Then Paul stood in the midst of the Areopagus and said, 'Men of Athens, I perceive that in all things you are very religious; [23]for as I was passing through and considering the objects of your worship, I even found an altar with this inscription: to the unknown god. Therefore, the One whom you worship without knowing, Him I proclaim to you.'"

3e. **Colossians 3:5:** "Therefore, put to death your members, which are on the earth: fornication, uncleanness, passion, evil desire and covetousness, which is idolatry."

4a. **Hebrews 11:17-19:** (NASB) "By faith Abraham, when he was tested, offered up Isaac, and he who had received the promises was offering up his only begotten *son*; [18]it was he to whom it was said, "In Isaac your descendants shall be called." [19]He considered that God is able to raise people even from the dead, from which he also received him back as a type."

4b. **James 2:21-23:** "Was not Abraham our father justified by works when he offered Isaac his son on the altar? [22]Do you see that faith was working together with his works, and by works faith was made perfect? And the Scripture was fulfilled which says, 'Abraham believed God, and it was accounted to him for righteousness.' [23]And he was called the friend of God."

4c. **Genesis 22:11-14:** God provided a ram

4d. **Deuteronomy 12:31:** "You shall not worship the LORD your God in that way; for every abomination to the LORD which He hates they have done to their gods; for they burn even their sons and daughters in the fire to their gods."

Chapter 2

The Truth Corner

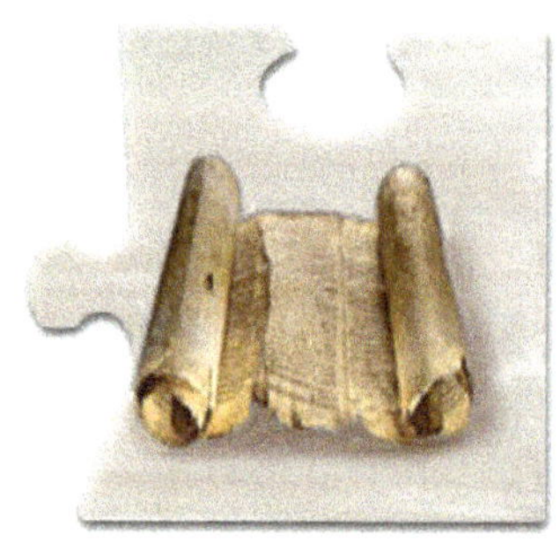

Many deny the existence of the truth puzzle piece. Others have it upside down or twist it to justify invalid pieces. Yet, that does not change the fact that objective truth exists and that we can know it. Since it is easy to twist our innate sense of right and wrong to justify our desires, we need a standard of truth higher than mankind. Finding a reliable source of truth is therefore the first critical step.

2.1 A Reliable Source

Over the ages, many have recorded their ideas and beliefs in sacred texts or holy books. A quick Internet search will list books for Hinduism, Buddhism, Sikhism, Baha'i, Islam, Scientism and hundreds more – each claiming to be the bearer of truth. One can find some truth in all of them. The real deal though will be the book that is set apart like a brilliant polished diamond amongst dull rocks. One with a central message unlike any other. Today, the Qur'an most likely takes second place amongst religious books, as Islam has slowly spread around the globe.

It all started around 632 AD, when an angel appeared to Mohammed in a cave and told him about Allah. Muhammad became a prophet and founded the religion of Islam. He was illiterate, so his companions most likely wrote down his words after his death. The collection of these works became known as the the Qur'an. However, copy errors and insertions soon created several versions with discrepancies. To solve the problem, the third caliph, Uthman, chose one of these versions to be the standard Qur'an for all Muslims, and destroyed the rest.[1]

The Qur'an describes miraculous events, some prophecies, information not generally known at that time, as well as many historical narratives similar to the Old Testament of the Bible.[2] Yet incongruities abound. Paramount is the fact that the Qur'an denies the deity of Christ and the triune nature of Jehovah God. Surah 4:171 states, "O People of the Scripture, do not commit excess in your religion or say about Allah except the truth. The Messiah, Jesus, the son of Mary, was but a messenger of Allah and His word which He directed to Mary and a soul [created at a command] from Him. So believe in Allah and His messengers. And do not say,

---

[1] S. Green, *The Preservation of the Qur'an.* <answering-islam.org/Green/uthman.htm>, accessed October 2015.

[2] T. Wallace, <fortressoffaith.org> accessed June 2015.

"Three"; desist - it is better for you. Indeed, Allah is but one God. Exalted is He above having a son."[1]

The Qur'an's assertion that Jesus was Mary's son, a true prophet and messenger from God, presents a dilemma. Jesus unmistakably claimed to be God the Son (Mark 14:60-65, John 8:58, John 14:7, see Chapter 5.2). If Jesus was only a messenger of Allah, then He was delusional or a liar and therefore not a true prophet or great moral teacher. The apostle Paul warned long before the Qur'an was written, "Beware lest anyone cheat you through philosophy and empty deceit, according to the tradition of men, according to the basic principles of the world, and not according to Christ." (Colossians 2:8) Perhaps, the most significant problem followers of Allah face is that apart from martyrdom, the Qur'an offers little guarantee to enter eternal paradise. In stark contrast, the God of the Bible does not require your death. Instead, He sent His own Son to die in your place.

The Bible, the Word of God, is widely regarded as the most read book in the world. This unique book claims an exalted position as the ultimate standard and authority on truth. It never relies or appeals to any other authority. Moses wrote, "God is not a man that He should lie." (Numbers 23:19) Jesus Christ himself declared, "I am the truth" (John 14:6) and John wrote, "God's word is truth." (John 17:17) Jesus also said God's word is the ultimate judge of truth (John 12:48). No truth exists apart from Him because in Him is hidden all the treasures of wisdom and knowledge (Colossians 2:3). According to the Bible, God gave all Scripture by His divine inspiration (2 Timothy 3:16). If this is true, the Bible must have unique and supernatural qualities. And it does!

God inspired over 40 men on three different continents for more than 1,500 years to write the 66 books of the Bible. They recorded history and prophecies, pronounced blessings and judgment, and answered countless questions according to God's instruction. Amongst the authors were kings, scholars, military men, shepherds and fishermen. Many were heroes with exceptional leadership, valiant men who changed history. Such were Moses, Daniel, King David, King Solomon and Paul, to name a few. Around 2000 years ago, soon after Jesus had conquered death, He personally called Saul of Tarsus into His service.

Saul, who became Apostle Paul, was a highly educated Roman citizen with a consuming passion for God. To protect God's holy name, he intensely persecuted the early Christians. That is until the day he met Jesus up close and personal and became a new man. Paul wrote many of the New Testament books and endured intense persecution and suffering, as he boldly proclaimed the truth until his death. It is said that Paul,

> has already influenced more minds than Plato ever did; in the end, he will have influenced far more than Plato, and Bacon, and Kant, and Locke,

---

[1] Qur'an, Surah 4. An-Nisaa, Ayah 171. Sahih International, <corpus.Qur'an.com>

> combined:— than all the Greek, the Persian, the Egyptian, the Roman priests and sages united. ... He travelled farther than Herodotus had done; he sought more than any other man the great central points of influence in the world; and at Jerusalem, at Damascus, at Antioch, at Ephesus, at Philippi, at Athens, at Corinth, at Rome, he left impressions of his presence and power such as no other man made, and destined to be of longer continuance than any opinions which influenced the men of that generation.[1]

Despite the variety of authors and times, all 66 books have a remarkable unity and central theme. They consistently point to the most important story, the one about God's plan for humankind that begins in the book of Genesis and concludes in the book of Revelation. Every book of the Bible expands on this plan, weaving the story with a continuous golden thread. No man or committee came together to plan it or oversee those taking part in the amazing story. No person could, since the authors (for the most part) lived in different times and never knew each other. Only someone who is greater than mankind and outside of time could have authored and executed this amazing plan. This awe-inspiring fact alone sets the Bible apart from any other book on the planet. It is however, not the only evidence to validate the Bible as the source of ultimate truth.

A myriad of external evidence confirms the Bible's reliability, such as archeologically verified places and events, extra-Biblical documents and scientific accuracy. Details on this are readily available from many sources.[1] Unlike the Qur'an, the factual consistency within the Bible and amongst the multiple copies thereof further points to divine guidance and preservation. The Bible is also a record of countless detailed prophecies that were fulfilled to the letter. More on this in the next chapter. The evidence of the divine inspiration of Scripture is truly overwhelming.

Sometimes parts of the Bible can be confusing at first glance, only because we lack knowledge of customs and places. For instance, in Revelations 3:15-16, God warns the church of Laodicea, "I know your works, that you are neither cold nor hot. I could wish you were cold or hot. So then, because you are lukewarm, and neither cold nor hot, I will vomit you out of My mouth." Would God wish anyone to be spiritually cold? No, but to the people of Laodicea the message was clear. The analogy referred to the water condition of the city of Laodicea, which was

---

[1] *Early Training of the Apostle Paul*, <biblestudytools.com/classics/barnes-scenes-in-life/early-training-of-the-apostle-paul.html>, accessed November 2015.

[1] For example, watch the fascinating and award-winning documentary, *Patterns of Evidence: Exodus*, by Timothy Mahoney. <patternsofevidence.com>.

[2] D. Padfield, *Churches In The Lycus River Valley In Turkey. The Church at Laodicea in Asia Minor.* <padfield.com/2005/laodicea.html>, accessed November 2015.

dependent on mineral rich water piped from a spring south of the city. By the time the water reached the city, it was lukewarm and nauseating. This was in stark contrast to the therapeutic hot springs of the nearby city Hierapolis and the refreshing cold water of Colossae.[2]

Some critics argue that even though the Bible is true, verifiable and reliable, man cannot accurately interpret it. However, this incorrect reasoning denies objective truth. Dr. Jonathan Sarfati, a creationist and chemist, explains, "The accuracy of interpretation of Scripture is determined by how it matches the intended meaning of the author. This is determined by rule of grammar and historical and literary context ... an appeal to general human fallibility is simply not sufficient."[1] Ultimately, only the life-changing power of the Bible will convince you of the truth.

The Bible is "living and powerful, and sharper than any two-edged sword, piercing even to the division of soul and spirit." (Hebrews 4:12) Through the Bible, God reveals truths not as mystical or religious ideas but as practical wisdom from a personal friend and counselor. While Jesus walked the earth, He often told stories about everyday life to confront heart issues. He knew his hearers would inevitably find themselves in the stories. When Jesus taught, he used common language in a gentle way, but His words have depths that demand a lifetime to explore.

No other book has ever been hated with such a fury. It must be because light erupts from every page, and darkness hates the light. Brutal persecution over millennia has failed to obliterate the Bible's message of hope, love and truth. This fact testifies to the incredible life-giving power and truth of God's Word. If you choose the Bible as your ultimate source of truth, you will be able to determine truth in every situation you face. You will find unimaginable treasures and genuine Life Puzzle pieces. Most importantly, you will meet your holy and righteous Creator and develop a relationship with Him.

"And he who has seen has testified, and his testimony is true; and he knows that he is telling the truth, so that you may believe." (John 19:35)

Your turn to dig deeper: The Truth

1. How is Allah and the Qur'an different from the LORD God and the Bible? (Watch the online discussion, *The Koran vs Genesis*[2])
2. Read 2 Timothy 3:16, one of the most important statements in the Bible. What does it mean that all Scripture is God-breathed, or inspired by God? (Also, read 1 Corinthians 2:13).

---

[1] J. Sarfati, Ph.D., *Refuting Compromise*. Master Books. 2004, 45.

[2] *The Koran vs Genesis*. Creation Magazine LIVE! 4-21, <creation.com/creation-tv>.

3. Why did God give us His written word? (Read 2 Timothy 3:16 again, also Isaiah 43:10 and 1 John 5:13).

4. What is the root problem of those rejecting the truth of the Bible? (Read Romans 1:18, Ephesians 4:17-18 and 2 Peter 3:5, 15-16).

5. Who and what will convince those who hear the truth? (Read 1 Corinthians 2:4 and Hebrews 4:12).

Answers from the Bible

2. **2 Timothy 3:16:** "All Scripture is inspired by God and profitable for teaching, for reproof, for correction, for training in righteousness."
   1 Corinthians 2:13: **"**These things we also speak, not in words which man's wisdom teaches but which the Holy Spirit teaches, comparing spiritual things with spiritual."

3. **Isaiah 43:10:** "'You are My witnesses,' says the Lord, 'And My servant whom I have chosen, That you may know and believe Me, and understand that I am He. Before Me there was no God formed, nor shall there be after Me.'"
   1 John 5:13: "These things I have written to you who believe in the name of the Son of God, that you may know that you have eternal life, and that you may continue to believe in the name of the Son of God."

4. **Romans 1:18:** "For the wrath of God is revealed from heaven against all ungodliness and unrighteousness of men who suppress the truth in unrighteousness."
   Ephesians 4:17-18: "This I say, therefore, and testify in the Lord, that you should no longer walk as the rest of the Gentiles walk, in the futility of their mind, [18]having their understanding darkened, being alienated from the life of God, because of the ignorance that is in them, because of the blindness of their heart."
   2 Peter 3:5: "For this they willfully forget: that by the word of God the heavens were of old, and the earth standing out of water and in the water."
   2 Peter 3:15-16: Peter warns that unstable people who don't know what they are talking about, twist Scripture to their own destruction.

5. **1 Corinthians 2:4:** "And my speech and my preaching were not with persuasive words of human wisdom, but in demonstration of the Spirit and of power, that your faith should not be in the wisdom of men but in the power of God."
   Hebrews 4:12: "For the word of God is living and powerful, and sharper than any two-edged sword, piercing even to the division of soul and spirit, and of joints and marrow, and is a discerner of the thoughts and intents of the heart."

2.2 Prophecies and Probabilities

Humans cannot foretell the future. Therefore, when prophesies come true it is powerful proof of divine origin. Unlike the vague prophesies of Nostradamus, the Bible is filled with detailed prophesies from the first one in Genesis 3, fulfilled in Christ Jesus, to the last ones in the book of Revelation, speaking of days in our near future. In this, the Bible is unique. Dr. Carl Broggi wrote, "There are no verified fulfilled prophesies in the Muslim's Koran, in the Latter Day Saint's Book of Mormon, in the Hindu's Upanishads or in any other religious or secular book."[1] Over a period of 1,500 years, many prophets, angels and regular people (like Joseph who interpreted dreams), accurately foretold events. Examples include the rise and fall of nations and kings, impending dangers and even weather forecasts.[2]

Most fascinating are the more than 300 prophesies about the birth, life, death and purpose of one person, the Lord Jesus Christ. Jesus himself claimed that the Scriptures testify about Him.[3] To put the significance of these prophesies in perspective, let us make up a modern day scenario. Imagine that around 1,500 years ago, several people accurately foretold some detail about Queen Elizabeth. Maybe they wrote where she would be born, the name of her great-great-great-grandfather, her role in England and world events, and in what manner she would die. This would be supernatural and surreal. However, much more than this was prophesied about Jesus, which is overwhelming evidence of the truth and divine inspiration of the Bible.

Critics say that the Lord Jesus, who knew the Old Testament, arranged events to fulfill prophesies, just so He could claim to be the Messiah. It is a bit difficult, however, to pre-arrange for example your own virgin birth, birthplace and crucifixion. Some say that you can find other historical figures that fit Messianic prophesies. It is true that certain individuals could fulfill one or even a few, but to find one person to fulfill them all is next to impossible. In the mid-1900s, Peter Stoner, a science professor, wanted to find out just how impossible this was. In his book, *Science Speaks*, he published a compilation of probability statistics regarding many prophesies, including those about Jesus. Members of the American Scientific Affiliation reviewed the mathematical analysis and found it sound, dependable and accurate.

Professor Stoner's initial assessment included only eight of the 300 prophesies regarding Jesus (listed in the question section below).[4] He found that the chance that any man fulfilled all eight prophesies was one in 10^{17}. This number is so

---

[1] C.J. Broggi, *Why is the Bible Unique?* In *How Do We Know the Bible is True?* Master Books. 2012, 55.

[2] Read Genesis 41, Daniel 8, Mathew 2:13, 1 Kings 17:1 as a few examples.

[3] Luke 24:44, John 5:39, Hebrews 10:7

[4] P. W. Stoner and R.C. Newman, *Science Speaks*. Moody Press Chicago, Online HTML revised edition 2002, Chapter 3, <sciencespeaks.dstoner.net>, accessed October 2015.

enormous and the chance so small, that Professor Stoner used an analogy to help the reader visualize it. He wrote,

> Suppose that we take 10^{17} silver dollars and lay them on the face of Texas. They will cover all of the state, two feet deep. Now, mark one of these silver dollars and stir the whole mass thoroughly, all over the state. Blindfold a man and tell him that he can travel as far as he wishes, but he must pick up one silver dollar and say that this is the right one. What chance would he have of getting the right one? Just the same chance that the prophets would have had of writing these eight prophecies and having them all come true in any one man, from their day to the present time, providing they wrote using their own wisdom.[1]

Perhaps you will agree at this point that this is as close to impossible that one can get, but Professor Stoner took it one step further by adding eight more prophesies, assuming the same probability as the first eight. This resulted in a chance of one in 10^{45}. The number 10^{45} is beyond comprehension, so Professor Stoner used another analogy to explain:

> Take this number of silver dollars. If you make these into a solid ball, you will have a great sphere with a center at the earth, and extending in all directions more than 30 times as far as from the earth to the sun. (If a train had started from the earth at the time the Declaration of Independence was signed, and had traveled steadily toward the sun at the rate of sixty miles per hour, day and night, it would be about reaching its destination today. But remember that our ball of silver dollars extends thirty times that far in all directions.) If you can imagine the marking of one silver dollar, and then thoroughly stirring it into this great ball, and blindfolding a man and telling him to pick out one dollar, and expect it to be the marked one, you have somewhat of a picture of how absolutely the fulfillment of sixteen prophecies referring to Jesus Christ <u>proves both that He is the Son of God and that our Bible is inspired</u>.

In his search for happiness and meaning, Josh McDowell tried religion, education, prestige and parties without finding answers. Eventually, he was drawn to a small group of Christian students at the university campus. Upon asking them why they are different, a student answered, "Jesus Christ." "Oh, for God's sake, don't give me that kind of garbage. I'm fed up with religion. I'm fed up with the church. I'm, fed up with the Bible," he snapped.[2] His new friends then pointed out that Christianity is not a religion. Religion is humans trying to work their way to God. They challenged him to make a "rigorous, intellectual examination of the claims of Christ," which is exactly what he did. He even suspended his studies for a period. Josh started by looking for "indisputable evidence that the Bible is unreliable." He found evidence, lots of it, but evidence that led him to the conclusion that "the Old and New Testament documents are some of the most reliable documents in all of

---

[1] P. W. Stoner and R.C. Newman, *Science Speaks*. Moody Press, Online HTML revised edition 2002, Chapter 3, <sciencespeaks.dstoner.net>, accessed October 2015.

[2] J. McDowell and S. McDowell, *More Than a Carpenter*. Tyndale. 1977, 2005, 2009, 5.

antiquity."[1] His wrote about his journey of finding true Life Puzzle pieces in his book, *More Than a Carpenter*. His story might just change yours.

Drawn by tales of rugged beauty and unique lifeforms, my husband and I decided to explore the Richtersveld, a harsh mountainous desert in South Africa. This was back in the days before cell phones and GPS devices. At the last remnant of civilization, a dusty town bordering the desert, we stopped to buy a map. Since roads were non-existent in the Richtersveld, the storeowner sold us a topographical map on which he signposted certain landmarks as well as places to avoid. That the map showed significant wear and tear after one week is an understatement. Our very lives depended on that map! Similarly, the Bible is the map for our life's journey. A journey filled with beauty and dangers alike. The Bible is the only accurate and trustworthy map available, because God, who cannot lie,[2] is the author. It is precious beyond words; treat it as such.

Your turn to dig deeper: Prophecies and Probabilities

1. Who is the ultimate source of prophesies recorded in the Bible? (2 Peter 1:21)

2. Jesus said, "These are the words which I spoke to you while I was still with you, that all things must be fulfilled which were written in the Law of Moses and the Prophets and the Psalms concerning Me." (Luke 24:44*)* Read eight of the 300 prophecies regarding Jesus Christ. These are the ones Professor Stoner used in his probability analysis.

	Prophecy	*Description*	*Fulfillment*
a.	Micah 5:2		Matthew 2:1-2
b.	Malachi 3:1		Luke 1:13-17
c.	Zachariah 9:9		Matthew 21:1-9
d.	Psalm 41:9		John 13:21-27
e.	Zechariah 11:12		Matthew 26:15
f.	Zechariah 11:13		Matthew 27:5-7
g.	Isaiah 53:7		Mark 15:3-5
h.	Psalm 22:16, Isaiah 53:12		Luke 23:33

[1] J. McDowell and S. McDowell, *More Than a Carpenter*. Tyndale. 1977, 2005 and 2009, 7.

[2] Titus 1:2, Isaiah 25:51

Answers from the Bible

1. **2 Peter 1:21:** "For prophecy never came by the will of man, but holy men of God spoke as they were moved by the Holy Spirit."

2a. **Micah 5:2:** "But you, Bethlehem Ephrathah, though you are little among the thousands of Judah, yet out of you shall come forth to Me the One to be Ruler in Israel, whose goings forth are from of old, from everlasting."

Matthew 2:1-2: "Now after Jesus was born in Bethlehem of Judea in the days of Herod the king, behold, wise men from the East came to Jerusalem, [2]saying, 'Where is He who has been born King of the Jews? For we have seen His star in the East and have come to worship Him.'"

2b. **Malachi 3:1:** "'Behold, I send My messenger, and he will prepare the way before Me. And the Lord, whom you seek, will suddenly come to His temple, even the Messenger of the covenant, in whom you delight. Behold, He is coming,' says the LORD of hosts."

Luke 1:13-17: "But the angel said to him, 'Do not be afraid, Zacharias, for your prayer is heard; and your wife Elizabeth will bear you a son, and you shall call his name John. [14]And you will have joy and gladness, and many will rejoice at his birth. [15]For he will be great in the sight of the Lord, and shall drink neither wine nor strong drink. He will also be filled with the Holy Spirit, even from his mother's womb. [16]And he will turn many of the children of Israel to the Lord their God. [17]He will also go before Him in the spirit and power of Elijah, to turn the hearts of the fathers to the children, and the disobedient to the wisdom of the just, to make ready a people prepared for the Lord.'"

2c. **Zechariah 9:9:** "Rejoice greatly, O daughter of Zion! Shout, O daughter of Jerusalem! Behold, your King is coming to you; He is just and having salvation, Lowly and riding on a donkey, a colt, the foal of a donkey."

Mathew 21:1-9, Jesus enters Jerusalem riding on a colt, the foal of a donkey.

2d. **Psalm 41:9:** "Even my own familiar friend in whom I trusted, Who ate my bread, Has lifted up his heel against me."

John 13:21, 25-27: "When Jesus had said these things, He was troubled in spirit, and testified and said, 'Most assuredly, I say to you, one of you will betray Me.' [25]Then, leaning back on Jesus' breast, he said to Him, 'Lord, who is it?' [26]Jesus answered, 'It is he to whom I shall give a piece of bread when I have dipped it.' And having dipped the bread, He gave it to Judas Iscariot, the son of Simon. [27]Now, after the piece of bread, Satan entered him. Then, Jesus said to him, 'What you do, do quickly.'"

2e. **Zechariah 11:12:** "Then I said to them, 'If it is agreeable to you, give me my wages; and if not, refrain.' So they weighed out for my wages thirty pieces of silver."

Matthew 26:15: "'What are you willing to give me if I deliver Him to you?' And they counted out to him thirty pieces of silver."

2f. **Zechariah 11:13:** "And the LORD said to me, 'Throw it to the potter'—that princely price they set on me. So I took the thirty pieces of silver and threw them into the house of the LORD for the potter."

Matthew 27:5-7: "Then he threw down the pieces of silver in the temple and departed, and went and hanged himself. [6]But the chief priests took the silver pieces and said, 'It is not lawful to put them into the treasury, because they are the price of blood.' [7]And they consulted together and bought with them the potter's field, to bury strangers in."

2g. **Isaiah 53:7:** "He was oppressed and He was afflicted, yet He opened not His mouth; He was led as a lamb to the slaughter, and as a sheep before its shearers is silent, so He opened not His mouth."

Mark 15:3-5: "And the chief priests accused Him of many things, but He answered nothing. [4]Then Pilate asked Him again, saying, 'Do You answer nothing? See how many things they testify against You!' [5]But Jesus still answered nothing, so that Pilate marveled."

2h. **Psalm 22:16:** "For dogs have surrounded Me; the congregation of the wicked has enclosed Me. They pierced My hands and My feet."

Isaiah 53:12: "Therefore, I will divide Him a portion with the great, And He shall divide the spoil with the strong, because He poured out His soul unto death, And He was numbered with the transgressors, and He bore the sin of many, And made intercession for the transgressors."

Luke 23:33: "And when they had come to the place called Calvary, there they crucified Him, and the criminals, one on the right hand and the other on the left."

Chapter 3

The Science Corner

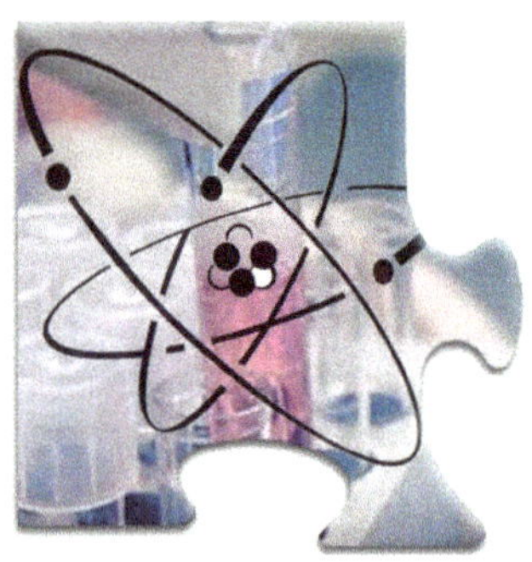

Scientists and the many branches of their studies fill the second corner of this puzzle. People often get riled up debating various issues of science. Perhaps this is because man is quite proud of his understanding of the universe and everything in it. When Charles Darwin published his book, *On the Origin of Species,* in 1859, it created a sensation. Here, finally, was a scientific puzzle piece to explain life without God. Today, secular scientists and the media claim that you must choose between science and God if you want to be intellectually acceptable, meaning that both beliefs cannot fit in the Life Puzzle. Before choosing, though, consider clarifying your ideas about science, scientists and the limits of scientific explanation.

3.1 Science

By definition, science is "the intellectual and practical activity encompassing the systematic study of the structure and behavior of the physical and natural world through observation and experiment."[1] This definition describes observational or operational science, which requires an eyewitness who gathers, interprets and publishes the data. It is repeatable and testable. A different kind of science exists that is not to be confused with observational science. It is called historical science and it relies only on indirect evidence. The indirect evidence used in historical science must always be interpreted, and the interpretation depends heavily on the assumptions or starting points of the scientist.

Historical science has produced origin theories such as the "Big Bang" (origin of the universe) and evolution (origin of species). Creationism is also an origin theory that explains God as the purposeful Creator of the universe and all life. Most people will categorize creationism as historical science. However, unlike the Big Bang and evolution theories, creationism is backed by an eyewitness account and reliable documentation.[2] By understanding that observational science is verifiable, but historical science depends on the scientist's assumptions, you can better sort through the good and the bad of the science puzzle pieces. Yet, depending on the nature of scientific fields, even observational science is not immune to interpretation and assumptions.

---

[1] The Oxford Dictionary.

[2] K. Ham and T. Mortenson, *Science or the Bible?* June 14, 2007, <answersingenesis.org>.

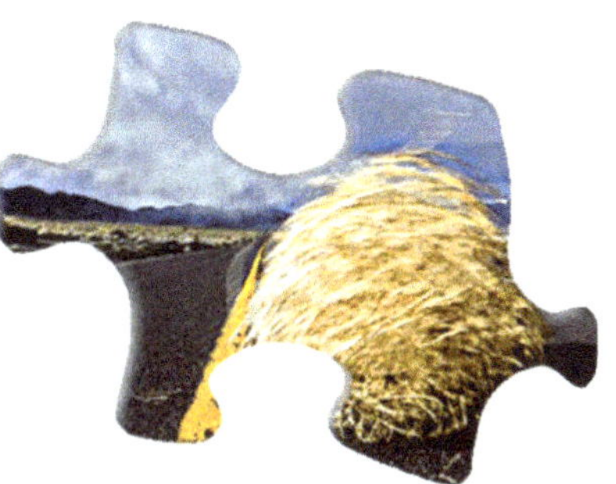

Fields of science such as astronomy and quantum physics are in constant flux as new research disproves or clarifies accepted facts. The reason lies, in part, in man's limited ability to explore deep space and the world of atoms respectively. The same is true for biology, medicine and nutrition, because the complexity of life is still far beyond our understanding. Many theories therefore resemble tumbleweeds – they stick to fences for a while, but eventually, they too roll away in the wind. This does not mean that science is a waste of time. On the contrary, it is critically important to save lives, improve living conditions, and to fulfill God's commandment to subdue the earth and rule the living creatures.[1]

Science is fascinating, and we enjoy the benefits of the resultant technology. It is rather chilling how much modern civilizations have come to depend on it. Yet, there is no ultimate precision and stability in man's scientific knowledge and understanding. S. M. Hutchens, the senior editor of *Touchtone*, wrote, "I am uneasy with the 'but science now understands' language used in support of theistic evolution. The current state of empirical [observational] science is too slender reed to lean on this way, since tomorrow it may 'understand' something much less friendly to theism."[2] Unlike scientific textbooks that quickly become obsolete, the Bible has stood the test of time. God's Word remains relevant, up-to-date and without mistakes.

"Who has directed the Spirit of the LORD, or as His counselor has taught Him?
[1]With whom did He take counsel, and who instructed Him, and taught Him in the path of justice? Who taught Him knowledge, and showed Him the way of understanding?" (Isaiah 40:13-14)

[1] Genesis 1:28

[2] S. M. Hutchens, *Review of Creation and Time by Hugh Ross.* Touchstone 8:40 Winter 1995.

Your turn to dig deeper: Science

1. A few thousand years ago, God questioned Job rather seriously in Job 38:4–7. Can you answer God?

2. Even though the Bible was not meant to be a science textbook, it contains many scientific truths. What was written regarding:
   a. The revolving earth? (Read Luke 17:34–36)
   b. Wind patterns? (Read Ecclesiastes 1:6)
   c. Washing in running versus stationary water for sanitizing purposes? (Read Leviticus 15:13)
   d. Sanitary legislation? (Read Leviticus 13)
   e. Four dimensions? (Read Ephesians 13:17-19. Note: In 1888, Charles H. Hinton coined the term "tesseract," to describe the four-dimensional analog of the cube.)

Answers from the Bible

1. **Job 38:4–7:** "Where were you when I laid the foundations of the earth? Tell Me, if you have understanding. [5]Who determined its measurements? Surely you know! Or who stretched the line upon it? [6]To what were its foundations fastened? Or who laid its cornerstone, [7]when the morning stars sang together, and all the sons of God shouted for joy?"

2a. **Luke 17:34–36:** (NASB) "I tell you, on that night there will be two in one bed; one will be taken and the other will be left. [35] There will be two women grinding at the same place; one will be taken and the other will be left. [36] Two men will be in the field; one will be taken and the other will be left."

2b. **Ecclesiastes 1:6:** "The wind goes toward the south, and turns around to the north; The wind whirls about continually, and comes again on its circuit."

2c. **Leviticus 15:13:** "And when he who has a discharge is cleansed of his discharge, then he shall count for himself seven days for his cleansing, wash his clothes, and bathe his body in running water; then he shall be clean."

2d. **Leviticus 13** provides sanitary legislation.

2e. **Ephesians 3:17-19:** (NASB) "... so that Christ may dwell in your hearts through faith; and that you, being rooted and grounded in love, [18] may be able to comprehend with all the saints what is the breadth and length and height and depth, [19] and to know the love of Christ which surpasses knowledge, that you may be filled up to all the fullness of God."

3.2 Scientists

As mentioned before, facts of science need interpretation. For example, Genesis 1:6-7 describes God's creation of a firmament. Fact: God created a firmament in the midst of the waters. Interpretation: the firmament was a water canopy. The interpretation always depends on the starting point of the author. Steven Hawkins admitted this when he wrote, "We are not able to make cosmological assumptions without some admixture of ideology."[1]

According to Thomas Kuhn, scientists often interpret data according to the ruling starting assumptions and models, easily explaining anomalies away.[2] Dr. Scott, an immunologist, wrote, "Even if all data points to an intelligent designer, such a hypothesis is excluded from science because it is not naturalistic."[3] Consensus, rather than truth, seems to be the driving force in the scientific community.

You also need to recognize when claims made by scientists are unfit for science puzzle pieces. For example, Richard Dawkins stated, "Only the scientifically illiterate believe we exist for a higher purpose. The scientifically literate know there is no reason 'why' we exist, we 'just do' as an accident of history."[4] This statement, while made by a credible scientist, is not a statement of science, but rather a statement of personal belief and opinion. "Statements from scientists are not always science!" warns Dr. Lennox.[5]

Furthermore, remember that all people, including scientists, are imperfect and deceitful by nature. Mistakes, whether intentional or not, abound. Be a critical reader with cordial skepticism. An article published in a peer-reviewed journal is likely to be more credible than a case study or opinion uploaded to the internet. Always insist on multiple sources of evidence and truthful examination before adding a science piece to your puzzle.

Some claim that you cannot be a real scientist and a Christian. This is another statement of opinion—and a false one at that. There are many internationally recognized Christian scientists, some with multiple doctoral degrees. They demonstrate excellence and integrity in their research, publish in scientific journals and are popular speakers at conferences. Consider also that many of the greatest

---

[1] S. W. Hawking and G.F.R Ellis, *The Large Scale Structure of Space Time.* Cambridge University Press. 1973, 134.

[2] T.S. Kuhn, *The Structure of Scientific Revolutions.* 3rd edition, University of Chicago Press. 1996.

[3] S.C. Todd, correspondence to *Nature.* 410 (6752):423, September 30, 1999.

[4] G. Easterbrook, *Of Genes and Meaninglessness.* Science. 277:892, August 15, 1997.

[5] J. Lennox, *Science and Faith.* 2013 Pensmore Dialogue.

scientists who ever lived made scientific breakthroughs, not in spite of, but because of their faith in the living Creator God.

These scientists expected to find laws, structure and ordered systems, because they served a God of order (See Chapter 3.6). Dr. Henry Morris writes, "And somehow this attitude did not hinder them in their commitment to the "scientific method." In fact, one of them, Sir Francis Bacon, is credited with formulating and establishing the scientific method! They seem also to have been able to maintain a proper "scientific attitude," for it was these men (Newton, Pasteur, Linnaeus, Faraday, Pascal, Lord Kelvin, Maxwell, Kepler, etc.) whose researches and analyses led to the very laws and concepts of science which brought about our modern scientific age."[1]

Most of us admire brilliance, whether we see it in a scientist, musician, artist, chef, athlete, engineer, or a leader. The list is endless, because people are amazing. However, all this admiration pales in comparison to the admiration due the greatest Scientist of all – the One who designed, built, and still maintains everything, from the tiniest molecular engine, to the vast incomprehensible galaxies. His mind and brilliance compare to none.

"To whom then will you liken Me, or to whom shall I be equal?" says the Holy One. Lift up your eyes on high, and see who has created these things, who brings out their host by number; He calls them all by name, by the greatness of His might And the strength of His power; not one is missing." (Isaiah 40:25-26)

Your turn to dig deeper: Scientists

1. Is it Biblical to be skeptical and demand evidence? Did people in the Bible ever ask for evidence from God? (Read Genesis 15:8-9, Numbers 16:28, Judges 6:17 and 2 Corinthians 8:24).
2. Why was the Berean believers called "fair-minded"? (Read Acts 17:11).
3. Does God require evidence from those who claim to be His children? (Read Matthew 7:15-20 and 2 Corinthians 13:5).
4. One of the Bible authors was a scientist called Luke.
   a. What was his occupation? (Read Colossians 4:14).
   b. Which two books did he write? (Read Luke 1:1-4 and Acts 1:1).
   c. From reading Luke 1:1-4, how thorough do you think his research was?
   d. Do you think he believed God created the universe and everything in it? (Read Acts 4:24).

---

[1] H. M. Morris Ph.D., *Bible-Believing Scientists of the Past.* <icr.org/article/bible-believing-scientists-past>.

Answers from the Bible

1. **Genesis 15:8-9:** "And he said, 'LORD God, how shall I know that I will inherit it?' So He said to him, 'Bring Me a three-year-old heifer, a three-year-old female goat, a three-year-old ram, a turtledove and a young pigeon.'"

   Numbers 16:28: "And Moses said: 'By this you shall know that the LORD has sent me to do all these works, for I have not done them of my own will.'"

   Judges 6:17: "Then he said to Him, 'If now I have found favor in Your sight, then show me a sign that it is You who talk with me.'"

   2 Corinthians 8:24: "Therefore show to them, and before the churches, the proof of your love and of our boasting on your behalf."

2. **Acts 17:11:** "These were more fair-minded than those in Thessalonica, in that they received the word with all readiness, and searched the Scriptures daily to find out whether these things were so."

3. **Matthew 7:15-20:** "Beware of false prophets, who come to you in sheep's clothing, but inwardly they are ravenous wolves. [16]You will know them by their fruits. Do men gather grapes from thorn bushes or figs from thistles? [17]Even so, every good tree bears good fruit, but a bad tree bears bad fruit. [18]A good tree cannot bear bad fruit, nor can a bad tree bear good fruit. [19]Every tree that does not bear good fruit is cut down and thrown into the fire. [20]Therefore by their fruits you will know them."

   2 Corinthians 13:5: "Examine yourselves as to whether you are in the faith. Test yourselves. Do you not know yourselves, that Jesus Christ is in you?—unless indeed you are disqualified."

4a. **Colossians 4:14:** "Luke the beloved physician and Demas greet you."

4b. **Luke 1:1-4:** "Inasmuch as many have taken in hand to set in order a narrative of those things which have been fulfilled among us, [2]just as those who from the beginning were eyewitnesses and ministers of the word delivered them to us, [3]it seemed good to me also, having had perfect understanding of all things from the very first, to write to you an orderly account, most excellent Theophilus, [4]that you may know the certainty of those things in which you were instructed.

   Acts 1:1: "The former account I made, O Theophilus, of all that Jesus began both to do and teach."

4d. **Acts 4:24:** "So when they heard that, they raised their voice to God with one accord and said: 'Lord, You are God, who made heaven and earth and the sea, and all that is in them.'"

3.3 Limits of Scientific Explanation

Underlying our willingness to accept scientific claims as fact, is a rising movement called "scientism." It is the idea that science is the only way to truth. Many renowned scientists would stake everything on the validity of that claim. Thankfully, the dangerous idea of scientism is false. To disprove it, Dr. Lennox uses logic. He said, "Is the statement that science is the only way to truth a statement of science? No, it is a statement about science. Thus, if it is not a statement of science and science is the only way to truth, that statement cannot be true. It must be false if it is true!"[1] Science cannot be the only way to truth, because there is truth that is outside the scope of science.

To explain, let us consider what science does. For example, the laws of gravity explain what gravity does and how it acts. The laws can give us equations to help send a man to the moon, but it cannot explain what gravity is. Explanation is limited even in science itself. Dr. Lennox uses the kettle to explain. He begins by asking, "Why is the kettle boiling?" Well, the stove heats up the kettle, which conducts energy and causes vibration of water molecules until it reaches 100 degrees Celsius. Nonsense! It is boiling because I want a cup of tea!

You see, there are two kinds of explanations: a "how" explanation and a "purpose" explanation. Science can only answer the how questions of function. It can explain the physical properties of paper and ink, but it cannot explain why the written letters or symbols such as music notes have meaning. A different level of explanation is needed, one of purpose and intelligence.[1]

Everyone admiring a beautiful mansion will naturally assume that a great architect designed it with purpose and intelligence. How then, can we look at the universe's intricate order and specific design, and not recognize the purpose and intelligence of the Architect? Sadly, too many reject the existence of a spiritual realm, despite the evidence from the physical realm.

Nicodemus, the Pharisee, once asked Jesus how a man could be reborn.[2] Jesus used earthly metaphors of birth and physical wind to explain spiritual rebirth, but Nicodemus still could not understand. Jesus then asked, "If I have told you earthly things and you do not believe, how will you believe if I tell you heavenly things?" (John 3:12) Jesus' question reveals the fact that science can never explain or define the spiritual realm. However, the physical realm clearly points to the almighty Creator in a way that not just scientists, but everyone, can see. Paul explained, "For

---

[1] J. Lennox, *Science and Faith.* 2013 Pensmore Dialogue.

[2] John 3:1-11

since the creation of the world, His invisible attributes are clearly seen, being understood by the things that are made, even His eternal power and Godhead, so that they are without excuse." (Romans 1:20)

"Have you not known? Have you not heard? The everlasting God, the LORD, the Creator of the ends of the earth, neither faints nor is weary. His understanding is unsearchable." (Isaiah 40:28)

Your turn to dig deeper: Limits of Scientific Explanation

1. Aristotle taught that a prime mover is a being solely responsible for creating the universe and everything in it. If a being has the power to create something out of nothing, will humans who are limited within the creation and bound to time be able to intellectually grasp the entirety and origin of this infinite Being? (Read Psalm 103:14, Isaiah 55:8-9 and 1 Corinthians 2:11).
2. Does God claim to be the prime or unmoved mover? (Read Colossians 1:16-17 and 1 Corinthians 8:6).
3. Daniel 3:8-28 tells of Shadrach, Meshach and Abednego, who refused to bow before the gold image of King Nebuchadnezzar, even though they were certainly familiar with the science of fire.
    a. Did they believe God was greater than the laws of nature?
    b. What reason did they give for their choice?
    c. What was Nebuchadnezzar's reaction?
4. God often overrules laws of nature, we call it miracles. You can find countless fascinating examples in the Bible. Below a few to consider. Some say the miracles in the Bible are only symbolic. What do you think? Does it matter?
    a. The water of the Jordan backed-up for the Israelites to cross over. (Joshua 3:14-17)
    b. The sun stood still. (Joshua 10:1-15)
    c. Balaam and the talking donkey. (Numbers 22:21-30)
    d. Jesus fed 5000 people with five loaves and two fish. (Matthew 14:13-21)
    e. Christ Jesus' resurrection. (1 Corinthians 15:3-8)

Answers from the Bible

1. **Psalm 103:14:** "For He knows our frame; He remembers that we are dust."
   Isaiah 55:8-9: "'For My thoughts are not your thoughts, nor are your ways My ways,' says the LORD. [9]'For as the heavens are higher than the earth, so are My ways higher than your ways, and My thoughts than your thoughts.'"
   1 Corinthians 2:11: (NASB) "For who among men knows the thoughts of a man except the spirit of the man which is in him? Even so the thoughts of God no one knows except the Spirit of God."

2. **Colossians 1:16-17:** "For by Him all things were created that are in heaven and that are on earth, visible and invisible, whether thrones or dominions or principalities or powers. All things were created through Him and for Him. [17]And He is before all things, and in Him all things consist."
   1 Corinthians 8:6: "... yet for us there is one God, the Father, of whom are all things, and we for Him; and one Lord Jesus Christ, through whom are all things, and through whom we live."

3. In **Daniel 3:8-28,** Daniel's friends disobey the king. You can find the book of Daniel after Ezekiel, between Psalms and the book of Matthew.

4a. **Joshua 3:14-17** describes the Jordan drying up because the water "rose in a heap very far away at Adam."
4b. **Numbers 22:21-30** tells of the pagan prophet Balaam, his conversation with his donkey and the Angel of the LORD.
4c. In **Matthew 14:13-21**, Jesus multiplied five loaves and two fish to feed 5000 people.
4d. **1 Corinthians 15:3-8:** "For I delivered to you first of all that which I also received: that Christ died for our sins according to the Scriptures, [4] and that He was buried, and that He rose again the third day according to the Scriptures, [5] and that He was seen by Cephas, then by the twelve. [6] After that He was seen by over five hundred brethren at once, of whom the greater part remain to the present, but some have fallen asleep. [7] After that He was seen by James, then by all the apostles.[8] Then last of all He was seen by me also, as by one born out of due time."

Science Puzzle Pieces

Before leaving the science corner of the puzzle, it will be helpful to sort through some of the puzzle pieces concerning the universe, rocks and fossils, organization and energy and lastly, life itself. A logical place to start is at the very beginning.

3.4 The Incredible Universe

• The Beginning

You are most likely familiar with the Big Bang theory and the singularity theories as explanations of the origin of the universe. With the help of great minds such as Newton, Robertson-Walker and Einstein, some astrophysicists determined that the universe is expanding. Reversing time, they make the assumption that space-time must have become a singular at the point S=0.[1] Alan Guth, the author of the inflation theory, wrote, "The observable universe could have evolved from an infinitesimal region. It's then tempting to go one step further and speculate that the entire universe evolved from literally nothing."[2] (Note that many scientists disagree, since they believe that a steady state universe always existed.[3]) However, there are several problems with the mind-boggling idea that a random expansion of nothingness created our universe.

First is the infinitely precise tuning of all forces to support the universe and life. For example, if the gravitational force were off just a bit either way, stars would burn up too fast or burn too cold. Martin Reese, a famous astrophysicist and cosmologist from England, wrote a book about six numbers and the universe. He concludes that:

> These six numbers constitute a 'recipe' for a universe. If any one of them were to be 'un-tuned,' there would be no stars and no life. Is this tuning a coincidence? Or is it the providence of a benign Creator? I take the view that it is neither. An infinity of other universes may well exist where the numbers are different. Most would be stillborn or sterile. We could only have emerged in a universe with the 'right' combination. It is astonishing that an expanding universe, whose starting point is so 'simple' that it can be specified by just a few numbers, can evolve (if these numbers are suitably 'tuned') into our intricately structured cosmos.[4]

Reese finds the data amazing, and he interprets it according to his starting point.

---

[1] S. W. Hawking, *The Large Scale Structure of Space Time*. Cambridge Univ. Press. 1973, 137.

[2] A. Guth and P. Steinhardt, *The Inflationary Universe*. Scientific American. May 1984, 128.

[3] F. Hoyle, G. Burbidge, and J.V. Narlikar, *A Different Approach to Cosmology.* UK: Cambridge University Press. 2000.

[4] M. Reese, *Just Six Numbers*: *The Deep Forces That Shape the Universe,* 2000.

Reese acknowledges that science cannot explain this fine-tuning, but he denies the existence of a spiritual reality. He chooses to believe in an untestable theory of an infinity of universes, which mirrors the reasoning behind evolution: something must eventually happen if you never quit trying. Like "the monkey banging away at the typewriter will eventually type a Shakespeare novel" argument. However, this argument lacks a critical component called "purpose." To explain, even if the monkey types for infinity, he can never reach a goal without a pre-determined purpose. Sir Reese's multi-verse theory, as well as the Big Bang theory, has no purpose whatsoever. These theories also lack an explanation of a source of energy.

Newton's first law of thermodynamics exposes the energy source problem. According to this law, energy cannot be created or destroyed. Scientists now agree that this law even holds true in quantum mechanics as well as the expanding universe.[1] Since new energy cannot be added to the universe, the universe must have received the total incalculable amount of energy at birth. Neither the multi-verse nor the Big Bang theory proponents have a testable answer for the original source of energy.

Dr. Sarfati lists a host of other problems with the Big Bang theory.[2] Quantized red shift analysis contradicts the no-center assumption. Star formation is another sticky issue. Gasses do not contract and spontaneously start a nuclear fusion reaction. It needs an unimaginable compression force. Some suggest exploding stars formed new stars, but how did the first star form? Missing antimatter, as well as problems in explaining galaxy formation and their rotations makes it difficult, if not impossible to link Big Bang pieces together.[2] These are not the only issues.

John Harnett writes, "Just detecting Cosmic Microwave Background (CMB) radiation, which was a big bang prediction of George Gamow in 1948, is not sufficient reason (evidence) to conclude that the big bang happened ...Besides there is contradictory evidence that supports the idea that the CMB radiation is not even from the background and thus it can't be leftover radiation from the big bang fireball, as is believed."[3] Recently, LIGO observatories observed gravitational waves as predicted by Einstein. Even though this exciting observation clarifies several theories, it does not strengthen the Big Bang theory in any way.[3]

On the other hand, Hebrews 1:10 explains, "In the beginning, LORD, you laid the foundations of the earth, and the heavens are the work of your hands." God Himself was the source of energy because He created the universe, as indicated by the Hebrew word *"bara"* in Genesis 1:1, 21, 27 and Genesis 2:3 and 4. *"Bara"* means

---

[1] Clara Moskowitz, *Fact or Fiction? Energy Can Neither Be Created Nor Destroyed.* Scientific American. August 5, 2014.

[2] J. Sarfati, *Refuting Compromise.* Master Books. 2004, Chapter 5.

[3] J.G. Hartnett, *What Impact Does the Detection of Gravitational Waves Have on Biblical Creation?* February 16, 2016, <creation.com>.

to shape or create which infers creating out of nothing. No person, not even the most brilliant scientist, can ever create out of nothing. So how did God create the universe out of nothing? Did you know the word "uni-verse" means "single spoken sentence?" The words "God said" in Genesis 1 represent God's action of creation, His "bara." Because energy equals matter,[1] we can conclude that God energized the universe creating time, matter and space with His spoken words.

Some claim that there are similarities between the Big Bang theory and Genesis 1. However, as long as the Big Bang tumbleweeds keep rolling, the future of any such similarities is in jeopardy. It makes infinitely more sense that the amazing cosmos reflects not random chaos, but rather the supreme intelligence and inexpressible ability of God, the Creator, as revealed in the Bible.

"He has made the earth by His power; He has established the world by His wisdom, and stretched out the heaven by His understanding." (Jeremiah 51:15)

The Milky Way in the starlit sky of West Texas[2]

---

[1] Albert Einstein, *Theory of Special Relativity,* $E=mc^2$.

[2] Photo courtesy of Steve Miller, <SteveMiller3D.com>.

Your turn to dig deeper: The Beginning

1. How did God create the universe? (Read Psalm 33:6-9, Jeremiah 51:15).
2. Our universe is in no way haphazard or illogical, and the laws of nature are constant. Would the universe then likely have originated from an unchanging source, or from random chaos? (Read James 1:16-18).
3. Everything, from the motion of planets to interactions between molecules to subatomic particles, obey laws of nature.
   a. Laws pre-suppose a lawgiver. Does God claim to be the lawgiver of the laws of nature (ordinances of heaven and earth)? (Read Jeremiah 33:25).
   b. Does the Bible provide a foundation for the laws of nature? (Read the article by Dr. J. Lisle, *God & Natural Law*. August 28, 2006, <answersingenesis.org/is-god-real/god-natural-law/>)
4. Is God bound to the laws and physical limits of the universe He created? (Read 1 Kings 8:27 and Isaiah 66:1).

Answers from the Bible

1. **Psalm 33:6-9**: "By the word of the LORD the heavens were made, and all the host
   of them by the breath of His mouth. [7] He gathers the waters of the sea
   together as a heap; He lays up the deep in storehouses. [8] Let all the earth fear
   the LORD; Let all the inhabitants of the world stand in awe of Him. [9] For He
   spoke, and it was done; He commanded, and it stood fast."

   Jeremiah 51:15: "He has made the earth by His power; He has established the world by His wisdom, and stretched out the heaven by His understanding."
2. **James 1:16-18:** "Do not be deceived, my beloved brethren. [17] Every good gift and
   every perfect gift is from above, and comes down from the Father of lights,
   with whom there is no variation or shadow of turning. [18] Of His own will He
   brought us forth by the word of truth, that we might be a kind of first fruits of
   His creatures."
3. **Jeremiah 33:25:** "Thus says the LORD: 'If My covenant is not with day and night, and if I have not appointed the ordinances of heaven and earth ... '"
4. **1 Kings 8:27:** "But will God indeed dwell on the earth? Behold, heaven and the highest heaven cannot contain You, how much less this house which I have built!"

   Isaiah 66:1: "Heaven is My throne, And earth is My footstool. Where is the house that you will build Me? And where is the place of My rest?"

• Age of the Universe

No one can go back to the beginning, and the snapshot we get during our lifetime cannot provide accurate information to determine the age of the earth. It is the same as attempting to tell the story of a movie by looking at one frame. The assumptions you have to make are enormous.

Moses wrote that God created everything in six literal days.[1] According to a literal interpretation of Genesis 1 and the Biblical genealogy records, the age of the universe totals to about 6,000 years. However, if the universe is only a few thousand years old, it should not be possible to see galaxies that are billions of light years away. Yet we do, which presents a problem. However, before dumping the young universe piece, consider the underlying assumptions in this statement:

- The assumption that theories about the space-time fabric of space are correct.
- The assumption that God limited Himself to create within the boundaries of the natural laws He set in place.

We cannot verify nor ignore these mammoth assumptions. If the assumptions are wrong, it changes everything.

God revealed the events of the Creation week, not as a scientific publication, but as a testament to His glory. Ultimately, we will have to ask Him one day to answer this question. The apostle Paul wrote, "For now we see in a mirror dimly, but then face to face; now I know in part ..." (1 Corinthians 13:12, NASB). Still, old-fashioned reasoning and available information may help you clarify your view on the age of the universe.

According to the Big Bang theory, the universe had its singular beginning around 14 billion years ago. Scientists determined this date based on many assumptions. They use the uniformitarianism piece, claiming that the same natural laws and processes that operate in the universe today have always operated in the universe in the past and apply everywhere in the universe. This is an unproven theory, and it is not the only one.

Some Christians believe the universe must be old because Satan and his minions needed time to rebel. In the early 1800s, Scottish theologian, Thomas Chalmers, suggested the "reconstruction-ruin" theory with an undetermined gap period between Genesis 1 verses 1 and 2. Satan rebelled sometime during this period, and as a result, God destroyed the "first world" with a flood, and completely remade the heavens and the earth. Supporters of this theory claims that 2 Peter 3:5-7 does not refer to Noah's flood, but to Genesis 1:2. Keep in mind that no one can know what

[1] Genesis 1 and Exodus 20:11

this "first world" looked like (whether God created life forms or not), or why God would have destroyed the physical world after Satan rebelled in heaven.

Though Pastor Chalmers did not use the "reconstruction-ruin" theory to match the earth's timeline to the secular interpretation of the fossil record, supporters of this theory do.[1] The debate continues. Two questions are worth considering: 1. Can we assume that the concept of time in the physical realm, matches that of the spiritual realm? If not, then the time needed for Satan to rebel becomes irrelevant. 2. Would any evidence of life (fossils) of the "first world" have survived God's proposed reconstruction of an earth that was "without form, and void"? (Genesis 2:1). Other theories deserving of further investigation has been proposed.

Scientists like Dr. R. Humphreys, Robert Gentry and J.K. West have postulated various theories to explain the distant starlight and young universe dilemma. They use models based on the general relativity theory, time distortion, shock waves and a rotating cosmos. Even though their aguments are sound and plausible, there is no final irrefutable theory, nor will there ever be.

This is not repeatable science, we are limited in our exploration of deep space, and our data are haunted by assumptions. Nevertheless, based on God's eyewitness account and reliable documentation by Moses, the young universe is an intellectually acceptable choice that fits other Biblical puzzle pieces effortlessly.

The Small Magellanic Cloud[2]

---

[1] *The Bible, Genesis and Geology*. < kjvbible.org/gap_theory.html>, accessed February 2016.

[2] Photo courtesy of NASA, ESA, and the Hubble Heritage Team (STScI/AURA) - ESA/Hubble Collaboration, News Release Number: STScI-2007-04. <hubblesite.org/newscenter>.

Your turn to dig deeper: Age of the Universe

1. How do we get true knowledge and wisdom? Note: Wisdom is knowledge girded by truth. (Read Proverbs 1:7 and Colossians 2:2-3).
2. The Bible contradicted many accepted ideas of its time. What does the Bible say about:
   a. The expansion of the universe? (Read Isaiah 40:22 and 44:24).
   b. Earth's position in space? (Read Job 26:7).
   c. The number of stars? (Read Genesis 15:5 and Psalm 147:4).
3. People have always studied the stars, and quickly figured out how to use them for navigation. One star of particular importance is mentioned in Matthew 2.
   a. Which one?
   b. What was its significance?
   c. In what peculiar ways did it shine and act?
   For historical background and in-depth explanations visit <bethlehemstar.com/setting-the-stage/the-nine-points-of-christs-star>

Answers from the Bible

1. **Proverbs 1:7:** "The fear of the LORD is the beginning of knowledge, but fools despise wisdom and instruction."
   Colossians 2:2-3: "... that their hearts may be encouraged, being knit together in love, and attaining to all riches of the full assurance of understanding, to the knowledge of the mystery of God, both of the Father and of Christ, [3] in whom are hidden all the treasures of wisdom and knowledge."

2a. **Isaiah 40:22:** "It is He who sits above the circle of the earth, and its inhabitants are like grasshoppers, who stretches out the heavens like a curtain, and spreads them out like a tent to dwell in."
Isaiah 44:24: "Thus says the LORD, your Redeemer, and He who formed you from the womb: 'I am the LORD, who makes all things, who stretches out the heavens all alone, who spreads abroad the earth by Myself;'"

2b. **Job 26:7:** "He stretches out the north over empty space; He hangs the earth on nothing."

2c. **Genesis 15:5:** "Then He brought him outside and said, 'Look now toward heaven, and count the stars if you are able to number them.' And He said to him, 'So shall your descendants be.'"
Psalm 147:4: "He counts the number of the stars; He calls them all by name."

3. **Matthew 2**: Wise Men from the East

3.5 Rocks, Fossils, Water and the Age of the Earth

Modern dating methods estimate the earth to be 4.54 billion years old. However, generations from Adam to Jesus Christ add up to only a few thousand years. So, either the earth is beyond ancient or it is very young. These two starting points usually lead to opposite explanations for geological formations. For example, there are two opposite ways to explain the formation of a canyon:

- a uniformitarian and old earth view holds that a little river slowly carved out the canyon over millions of years.
- a Biblical and young earth view explains that tons of water gushing seaward sometime after the flood, gouged the canyon within a short period.

The Pease River in West Texas.[1]

Both puzzle pieces cannot fit; you will have to choose. No need to flip a coin, there are plenty of fascinating evidence to examine in dating methods, the fossil record and geological formations.

• Dating Methods

Dating methods are the windows to the past or the "clocks in the rocks." All numerical dating methods for rocks and fossils involve counting of decaying radioactive isotopes in the sample, hence the name "radiometric dating." Not all types of rocks and fossils have these isotopes, so geologists often use dateable ones to relatively date objects close-by. Everything, therefore, depends on the accuracy of the radiometric dating.

Radiometric dating hinges on the fact that atoms prefer to be in a stable condition. Through a process called "radioactive decay," parent (unstable) isotopes change over time at a measurable rate into daughter (stable) isotopes; not like tooth decay, just forming a completely different element. For example, uranium

---

[1] Photo courtesy of Dr. M. Meintjes.

changes into lead, potassium into argon and rubidium into strontium in igneous rocks.[1] First, specialized equipment measures the parent and daughter isotopes in the sample. Then, geologists use the rate of decay to calculate the time it should have taken for the unstable parent atoms to change into the stable daughter atoms measured in the sample.

Of all the radiometric dating methods, people are most familiar with radiocarbon (Carbon-14) dating. They often assume that geologists use the carbon method to date rocks at "millions of years." However, herein lies two critical errors. First, the carbon dating method cannot date rocks, but only objects that contain carbon and that were once alive, like certain fossils. Secondly, unstable carbon-14 isotopes decay rapidly into the stable nitrogen-14. This rate of decay is expressed in terms of the half-life of carbon. The half-life of any radioactive material is the time it takes for half a given quantity of a radioactive element to decay. Carbon's half-life is only 5,730 years. Therefore, carbon dating can only date plants and animals that died thousands and not millions of years ago.[2]

The chemical analysis of a suitable sample is usually accurate and straightforward. The problem comes, once again, with assumptions when interpreting the data or reading the "clock." When you look at a clock to tell the time, you assume someone set it correctly to begin with, and that it is keeping time at a constant speed. In the same way, a geologist must make important assumptions when reading the rock clock. According to creation scientist Dr. Snelling, when dating rocks, geologists make the following assumptions:

- The sample's initial composition: Geologists assume there were no daughter isotopes when the rock formed; however, it is impossible to verify initial conditions.
- The source of isotopes: Geologists assume that no outside forces such as flowing water contaminated the sample, and that no leakage out of the sample occurred.
- The rate of decay: Geologists assume the rate of decay has been constant over millions of years. This is because physicists have measured the decay rates in laboratories over many decades and have found them to be constant. They also could not change it with heat, pressure, electrical or magnetic fields. New

[1] Igneous rocks form through cooling of lava or magma, e.g. granite and basalt.

[2] Dr. A. A. Snelling, *Carbon-14 Dating, Understanding the Basics*. October 1, 2010, <answersingenesis.org>.

evidence, however, indicates changing decay rates in the past.[1] No one can account for initial planetary conditions or cataclysmic events such as Noah's worldwide flood with volcanic eruptions, simply because it is impossible to recreate such conditions.[2]

If the above assumptions are correct, then the dating results should be accurate. However, verification is simply impossible. Because dating methods rely heavily on these assumptions, the reliability decreases with an increase in the estimated age.

In a spectacular display of tremendous power, Mount St. Helens blew her top in 1980. Twelve years later, Dr. Austin selected a newly formed rock from the lava dome and sent crushed pieces to a highly reputable laboratory. The results? The lab estimated ages of the samples from 340,000 to 2.8 million years, not 12 years. This and many other similar examples underscore the unreliability of the clocks in the rocks.[3]

It is therefore reasonable to doubt ages of millions of years claimed by scientists. The Bible, in contrast, gives detailed descriptions of events and genealogies from day one. Many scholars have spent years adding numbers and verifying the accuracy of Biblical records by comparing it with other historical documents. They estimate the age of Earth to be around 6,000 years old. Even considering the debate regarding possible gaps in the genealogy records, the idea of millions of years is glaringly absent among the pages of the Bible.[4]

Your turn to dig deeper: Dating Methods

Those searching for a puzzle piece to link millions of years and the Bible, proposed that there are gaps in Biblical genealogies. The most common argument is that if there are gaps in <u>some</u> of the genealogies, there must be gaps in the <u>Old Testament</u> genealogies. This means that we can not accurately determine the age of the earth based on Biblical data.

1. A few of the genealogies do contain gaps, such as in Mathew's version of Christ's genealogy. (Compare 1 Chronicles 3:11-14 with Matthew 1:8.)
   a. What was the relationship between Joram and Uzziah (a.k.a. Azariah)? Note: It was acceptable practice for Jews to call a grandfather "father," or grandson, "son."
   b. Does Mathew's genealogy version definitively prove that there must be gaps in the Old Testament genealogies?

---

[1] For more information read D. DeYoung, *Thousands... Not Billions*. Master Books. 2005, 65-78.

[2] Dr. A. A. Snelling, *Radiometric dating: Back to Basics.* June 17, 2009, <answersingenesis.org>.

[3] K. Swenson, *Radio-Dating in Rubble*. Creation *23,* no 3 (June 2001): 23-25.

[4] J. Lisle and T. Chaffey, *Are There Gaps in the Genesis Genealogies? Appendix C.* March 22, 2012, <answersingenesis.org>.

2. Some try to add gaps in the Genesis genealogy at the time when people lived for hundreds of years. (Read Genesis 5).
   a. How many generations are there from Adam to Noah?
   b. How many years from Adam until Noah was 500 years old? The table gives the age of each father at the birth of their son for the first 10 generations on earth.

1. Adam	130
2. Seth	105
3. Enosh	90
4. Cainan	70
5. Mahalaleel	65

6. Jared	162
7. Enoch	65
8. Methuselah	187
9. Lamech	182
10. Noah	500

   c. What did Jude say about Enoch and Adam? (Read Jude 14).
   d. Do you see evidence for gaps?

3. Jude 14 claims that Enoch was a prophet. What may Enoch have foretold when he named his son "Methuselah?" Note that in Hebrew, "Methuselah" means, "When he dies, it shall be sent."[1]
   a. How old was Methuselah when he died? (Read Genesis 5:27).
   b. How old was Noah when the flood came? (Read Genesis 7:6).
   c. Did Methuselah die in the year of the flood? (Add ages from Methuselah to Noah's age at the flood: 187, 182 and 600).

Answers from the Bible

1. **Chronicles 3:11-14:** "Joram his son, Ahaziah his son, Joash his son, [12] Amaziah his son, Azariah his son, Jotham his son, [13] Ahaz his son, Hezekiah his son, Manasseh his son, [14] Amon his son, and Josiah his son."
   Matthew 1:8: "Asa begot Jehoshaphat, Jehoshaphat begot Joram, and Joram begot Uzziah."

2. **Genesis 5:** The family of Adam

2c. **Jude 14:** "Now Enoch, the seventh from Adam, prophesied about these men also, saying, 'Behold, the Lord comes with ten thousands of His saints.'"

3a. **Genesis 5:27:** "So all the days of Methuselah were nine hundred and sixty-nine years; and he died."

3b. **Genesis 7:6:** "Noah was six hundred years old when the flood waters were on the earth."

---

[1] Jonathan Sarfati, *Refuting Compromise*. Master Books. 2004, 296.

• Fossils

Fossils tell intriguing stories of the distant past. Some give us a glimpse of unusual creatures that once roamed the earth and others are quite familiar. Few fossils created such a stir as the huge fossil bones found since the 1600s. It was not until 1841 that British scientist Richard Owen came to realize that such fossils were so distinct from any living creature, that they deserved their own name. Owen promptly labeled them "*dinosauria*," which means "terrible lizards."

Over the years, many more fossils surfaced in different layers or geological strata. Eventually, scientists compiled the standard geological time scale from an uniformitarian starting point. The layers, they said, represent millions of years with abrupt changes in animal life between the layers. They found the "primitive" creatures in the lower and oldest rock layers, and found the more evolutionary or "advanced" ones in higher layers. The media and most scientists present this time scale as fact. However, there is more to the story. The combination of layers and fossils as presented in the standard geological time scale is theoretical. You can only find sections of it at any one location.

Noah's worldwide flood[1] presents a different explanation for the majority of fossil formation. During the flood, animals were catastrophically buried in layers of mud laid down in quick succession. This created ideal conditions for fossil formation on a large scale. The "primitive" life forms found in the lower layers are mostly stationary and the more "advanced" creatures are in higher levels, simply because they could run to higher grounds to escape rising water during the flood. From this starting point, the abrupt changes between kinds of life forms in different layers are easy to explain. Polystrate tree fossils (trees that stand upright across layers) also indicate rapid deposition of multiple layers rather than long ages between layers.[2]

Despite occasional claims of "missing link" fossils, the fossil record lacks the abundance of in-between fossils needed for incremental evolution between kinds. The few unaltered missing link fossils found could have been extinct species not fitting into any man-made class. For example, the unusual (but fascinating) duckbill platypus of Australia will make a great missing link fossil because it has characteristics of both a mammal and a bird. Most fossils show that nothing, in fact, has changed. Scientists beieved that the coelacanth fish and Wollemi pines had been extinct for millions of years, until live specimens showed up without any

---

[1] Genesis 6-7. Read more about Noah's flood in the "Water and Ice" section.

[2] Dr. John Morris, *Chapter 9 Do Fossils Show Signs of Rapid Burial?* December 30, 2013. <answersingenesis.org>

evolutionary changes. Fossils of bats, shrimp, lobsters, nautilus, crabs, sea horses, dragonflies, mosquitoes and ferns, dated as millions of years old, also show no sign of evolutionary changes when compared with live specimens.

Fossils can only form when tons of mineral-rich mud rapidly buries an animal. Because of the tremendous sheer forces during the burial process, it is rare to find intact fossils of larger animals. Geologists must piece the scattered bones together and sometimes use a lot of imagination regarding the anatomy of the creature they discovered. It is therefore no surprise that new fossil finds enable geologists to correct earlier errors and improve the accuracy of the specimens. Often, a fossil claimed to be an ape-man, turns out to be a child or a monkey, or a dinosaur skull finally finds its true bones. Fossils, however, are not the only images we have of ancient creatures.

Even though the term "dinosaur" was coined only a few hundred years ago, ancient documents describe terrible lizards or dragons in detail. They have been the stuff of legends amongst all nations as long as man has lived. According to the geological scale, dinosaurs became extinct before mankind evolved. Did it ever strike you as odd that man knew so much about them before they discovered the first dinosaur bones? Genesis 7 describes the terrible flood that destroyed all earthbound living things. This included gigantic, thousand-year-old dinosaurs. However, the young ones who disembarked on the ark had enough time to multiply and grow into the majestic beasts God referred to when He spoke to Job, who lived 300-400 years after the flood.[1]

Yet, in order to accommodate the geological column of fossils, some Christian theologians fit millions of years between Genesis 1 verse 2 and 3, when the earth was formless, empty and dark. They call this idea the "gap theory." Progressive creationists have a different approach.[2] They propose that God created everything in six literal days, but that He waited long periods between the actual days of creation. This is called the "soft gap theory." They reason, for example, that land cannot produce seed-bearing plants in one day. To support the soft gap theory, they argue that the Hebrew text of Genesis 1 uses the article "a" instead of "the" for the first five days, making the days generic and not consecutive.

---

[1] G. L. Bartholomew, *Dating the Book of Job.* <ancient-hebrew.org/docs/39_job.pdf>.

[2] Dr. J. C. Lennox, *Seven Days That Divide the World: The Beginning According to Genesis and Science.* Zondervan. 2011.

Yet sentences have multiple words to convey intended meaning of the author, and you have to consider <u>all</u> the words for accurate interpretation.[1] The soft gap theory has other problems as well. For example, it cannot explain how plants survived millions of years without insects and animals to pollinate flowers and disperse seeds. The plants also had to multiply without the seasonal and gravitational effects of the sun and moon.

Another view is the "framework hypothesis." Proponents of this theory claim that one should not interpret Genesis 1:1-2:3 literally. They view the Genesis account as topical picture frames in a story, not to be taken in order. In his book, *As It Is Written. The Genesis Account Literal or Literally?* (Master Books, 2016), Dr. Kenneth Gentry provides a clear detailed analysis, as well as powerful refutation of this theory.

With each of the days quantified by "morning and night," it is most likely that Moses intended to mean one Earth week.[1] Also, when God gave Moses the Ten Commandments, He clearly confirmed the intended meaning, "For in six days the LORD made the heavens and the earth, the sea, and all that is in them ... " (Exodus 20:11)

We cannot know exactly what happened those many years ago apart from what God revealed to us. We do know all humans function optimally with a six-day workweek followed by one day of rest. We seem to be wired that way. Science cannot disprove Genesis 1. On the contrary, an abundance of scientific data supports the fact that animals have always existed according to their kinds. Alas, problems with dating methods, fossil reconstruction and a lack of cameras thousands of years ago, leave us mostly with speculation when telling the stories of the fascinating creatures caught in time.

Your turn to dig deeper: Fossils

1. Did you know there are dinosaurs in the Bible? They just have different names such as "behemoth." However, some newer Bible versions translate the Behemoth in Job as a hippopotamus or an elephant. (Read Job 40:15-19).
    a. What descriptions rule out hippos or elephants as candidates?
    b. Could it have been a creature that became extinct later on as result of loss of habitat? Think gigantic dinosaur, like a titanosaur. Think about how much food these animals required and how devastating droughts would have been for their survival.

2. Some versions translate the Leviathan (ןינת, tannin in Hebrew) as a crocodile or whale. (Read Job 41).

---

[1] J. Sarfati, *Refuting Compromise*. Master Books. 2004, Chapter 2. You can also read a review of Dr. John Lennox' book by S. Turpin, June 27, 2012 at <answersingenesis.org>.

a. Even though crocodiles kill people, men can catch them with a rope. What other descriptions rule out crocodiles and whales?
b. The name "Leviathan" appears in other places in the Bible as well. It mostly refers to some kind of reptilian creature. (Read Job 3:8, Psalm 104:26 and Isaiah 27:1).[1] Do any sound familiar?
c. Compare the Leviathan to that of the colossal ancient marine reptiles like plesiosaurs.[2]

Answers from the Bible

1. **Job 40:15-19:** "Look now at the behemoth, which I made along with you; He eats grass like an ox. [16] See now, his strength is in his hips, and his power is in his stomach muscles. [17] He moves his tail like a cedar; the sinews of his thighs are tightly knit. [18] His bones are like beams of bronze, His ribs like bars of iron. [19] He is the first of the ways of God; Only He who made him can bring near His sword."

2. **Job 41:** God, Job and the power of the Leviathan.

2b. **Job 3:8:** "May those curse it who curse the day, those who are ready to arouse Leviathan."

Psalm 104:26: "There the ships sail about; there is that Leviathan which you have made to play there."

Isaiah 27:1: "In that day the LORD with His severe sword, great and strong, will punish Leviathan the fleeing serpent, Leviathan that twisted serpent; and He will slay the reptile that is in the sea."

A coyote trying to mess with the Texas horned lizard (above) may get a nasty surprise. These mini-dragons can accurately shoot streams of blood with repellant chemicals from the corners of their eyes![3]

---

[1] K. Ham and T. Chaffey, *Tannin: Sea Serpent, Dinosaur, Snake, Dragon, or Jackal?* August 8, 2012, <answersingenesis.org>.

[2] For more information, read *Meet Leviathan.* October 31, 2009, <answersingenesis.org>.

[3] *Blood Squirting Lizard.* National Geographic, <youtube.com>. Photo courtesy of Dr. M. Meintjes.

• Other Geological Evidence

If the earth is young, then there must be plenty of geological evidence to support the claim. Dr. Andrew Snelling explains that there is too little sediment on the seafloor and too little salt in the sea for a planet supporting life for millions of years. The earth's magnetic field also decays too rapidly.[1] He further points out that, "In many mountainous areas, rock layers thousands of feet thick have been bent and folded without fracturing. How can that happen if they were laid down separately over hundreds of millions of years and already hardened?"[2]

Cliffs at Big Bend National Park show the bending of layers.[3]

The bending of layers is still controversial, but it is reasonable to accept that the unbroken, bent rock layers like those in the photo above were folded while still somewhat pliable. Only a global, cataclysmic flood could carry the massive layers of sediment across continents as we see it today and lay it down in layers. The bending could have occurred during post flood tectonic activity. Nevertheless, many claim that massive cave formations undeniably tell the story of millions of years.

Stepping down clammy walkways into the bowels of the earth is a fascinating experience. Dark, limestone caves with low lights that highlight fascinating shapes of cave needles, gypsum flowers, slender stalactites and fat stalagmites add to the surreal effect. The tour guide always asks you not to touch the delicate formations,

---

[1] A.A. Snelling, *10 Best Evidences From Science That Confirm a Young Earth.* October 1, 2012, <answersingenesis.org>.

[2] A.A. Snelling, *Rock Layers Folded, Not Fractured, Flood Evidence Number Six.* April 1, 2009, <answersingenesis.org>.

[3] Photo courtesy of Dr. M. Meintjes.

since it took millions of years to grow them. While it is true that the oils and dirt on your fingers will cause damage, the claims about old age are open to debate.

Some geologists believe that dead marine animals in shallow salt seas sank to the sea floor 300 million years ago. Their skeletons turned into hundreds of feet of limestone. After millions of years of burial under sediment, water slowly eroded the limestone to form caverns. Geologists use radiometric dating when possible, but they also assume that the rate of cave formation observed today is the same as it was when these caves originally formed. This means the water flow and the mineral content of the water must have stayed the same for all the millions of years.

This is highly unlikely, since major changes have been observed just in the past few centuries. Also, keep in mind that limestone formations can grow very quickly under the right conditions. For example, the historic Cape Leeuwin waterwheel (top right photo)[1] was built in 1895 for the lighthouse keepers. It became stuck in rock and time in less than 100 years.

Most of the major limestone layers in caves also do not resemble the slow accumulation of dead marine sediment, but rather enormous twisted layers with animals buried catastrophically. A global flood followed by tectonic activity can easily explain majestic caves[2] such as the Carlsbad Caverns in New Mexico and the Flute Caves of China, (bottom right photo).[3]

"Lift up your eyes to the heavens, and look on the earth beneath. For the heavens will vanish away like smoke, the earth will grow old like a garment, And those who dwell in it will die in like manner; but My salvation will be forever, and My righteousness will not be abolished." (Isaiah 51:6)

---

[1] Photo courtesy of Michael Skovron, <mikeandcarolskovron.blogspot.com>, November 1, 2008.

[2] M.J. Oard, *Rapid Cave Formation by Sulfuric Acid Dissolution.* December 1, 1998, <answersingenesis.org>.

[3] Rainbow-Colored Reed Flute Caves of Guilin, China. Photo courtesy of Dr. M. Meintjes.

Your turn to dig deeper: Other Geological Evidence

1. How does the Bible explain the origin of Earth's water? (Read Genesis 1:2-10 and 2 Peter 3:5). Note that the Hebrew translation for the word "deep" refers to ocean depths or deep water.

2. Did Jesus believe in a young Earth?
   a. What did Jesus say about people in the beginning? (Read Mark 10:6).
   b. The Bible never recorded Jesus using Adam's name, only Abel, Adam's son. Did Jesus acknowledge Abel as a real or figurative person? (Read Luke 11:50-51).

Answers from the Bible

1. **Genesis 1:2-10**: (NSAB) "The earth was formless and void, and darkness was over the surface of the deep, and the Spirit of God was moving over the surface of the waters. [3] Then God said, 'Let there be light'; and there was light. [4] God saw that the light was good; and God separated the light from the darkness. [5] God called the light day, and the darkness He called night. And there was evening and there was morning, one day. [6] Then God said, 'Let there be an expanse in the midst of the waters, and let it separate the waters from the waters.' [7] God made the expanse, and separated the waters which were below the expanse from the waters which were above the expanse; and it was so. [8] God called the expanse heaven. And there was evening and there was morning, a second day. [9] Then God said, 'Let the waters below the heavens be gathered into one place, and let the dry land appear'; and it was so. [10] God called the dry land earth, and the gathering of the waters He called seas; and God saw that it was good."
   2 Peter 3:5: (NSAB) "For when they maintain this, it escapes their notice that by the word of God the heavens existed long ago and the earth was formed out of water and by water,"

2a. **Mark 10:6:** "But from the beginning of the creation, God 'made them male and female.'"

2b. **Luke 11:50-51:** "... that the blood of all the prophets which was shed from the foundation of the world may be required of this generation, [51] from the blood of Abel to the blood of Zechariah who perished between the altar and the temple. Yes, I say to you, it shall be required of this generation."

• Water and Ice

The abundance of Earth's water is likewise difficult to explain with the naturalistic starting point. Planetary scientists used to think that the water came from material that formed Earth billions of years ago, and that it condensed into oceans right away. However, about 30 years ago, a theory stating that a grazing impact by a Mars-sized body knocked off a piece of rock that became the moon, gained popularity. Taking a chunk out of our planet would have vaporized and removed any primordial oceans, leaving behind a parched earth. Hence, scientists proposed other theories for the origin of Earth's water to include thousands of comets striking earth; an unlikely source because the hydrogen isotope ratios of Earth's water do not match those of various comets. Others suggest that the water likely came from asteroids.[1]

In contrast, the Bible speaks of the abundance and importance of water from the first day of creation. It also describes, in detail, a worldwide flood about 2,000 years later. Some insist that the tale of Noah's ark and the flood, as described in Genesis 5-9, was just a tale of epic proportions. Pictures portray the ark as a bathtub toy. Recent scientific studies confirm the seaworthiness of the ark, a vessel the size of a cargo ship.[2] Others show that the animals could easily fit[3] and survive the wild ride when the rain started pouring and the "fountains of the deep broke open" (Genesis 7:11). According to Genesis 5 and 6, Noah was a real person, a tenth-generation baby who grew up to be a righteous man who walked with God. When we take Noah's story as a historical event, then all the geological puzzle pieces fall in place.

This includes cataclysmic tectonic plate activity, the Ice Age, sedimentary layers that cover continents and, as Ken Ham from *Answers in Genesis* puts it, "the millions of dead things buried in rock layers laid down by water, all over the earth." Have you ever considered our modern life without a worldwide flood, which buried enormous forests to produce fossil fuels (oil, gas, coal)? No cars, electricity, plastic, cell phones ... gasp! Only a global flood can account for the abundance and geographical distribution of fossil fuels and fossils we dig up today.[4] Only a global flood could have triggered an Ice Age.

The Ice Age was a time of extensive glacial activity covering up to 30 percent of the land. The secular uniformitarian theories propose many such periods that began

---

[1] D. Faulkner, *The Evolving History of the Earth's Oceans.* March 17, 2015, <answersingenesis.org>.

[2] T. Lovett, *Thinking Outside the Box.* March 19, 2007, <answersingenesis.org>.

[3] M. Ross, *No Kind Left Behind, Recounting the Animals on the Ark.* January 1, 2013, <answersingenesis.org>.

[4] N. Chartier, *Does the Fossil Record Prove Evolution?* <accordingtothescriptures.org>, accessed August 2015.

about 2.6 million years ago. However, these theories do not explain what triggered the Ice Age(s). Many scientists today are convinced that the geologic evidence points to a single Ice Age that formed after the flood and lasted around 700 years.[1]

A brief summary of the Ice Age theory that fits the Biblical account of the flood, is as follows. The global volcanic events that accompanied the breaking open of the fountains of the oceans had a two-fold effect: 1. Volcanoes spewed enough ash into the atmosphere to block sunrays, which lowered atmospheric temperatures. 2. Volcanic activity heated up the oceans, causing increased evaporation that accumulated as snow and ice over the Polar Regions. The ice could not melt because of lower atmospheric temperatures, and massive ice sheets extended downwards from the poles. The ice sheets, however, never reached as far as the flourishing civilizations at the lower latitudes, where the ark landed. Because so much water was trapped at the poles, the ocean levels dropped for centuries after the flood. The exposed land formed bridges for animals and people to cross over to different continents.

The evidence for a young planet is measurable and rational. The geological record does not disprove the Bible. On the contrary, it supports and confirms it. Rock formations and fossil records as a graveyard of Noah's flood, makes infinitely more sense than an uniformitarian theory of slow changes over millions of years.

Your turn to dig deeper: Water and Ice

1. What happened to the earth's water during the flood? Do you think the ark had a quiet ride? (Read Genesis 7:11-12 and 18-19).
2. Did other writers regard Noah as a real person? (Read Ezekiel 14:14, Hebrews 11:7 and 2 Peter 2:5).
3. Will there be another worldwide flood? What sign did God give? (Read Genesis 9:11-13).
4. The Bible recorded the history of people in Jesus' genealogy written in Luke 3:23-37. Knowing where they lived, explains why the Bible does not mention the Ice Age.[2]
    a. Which son of Noah followed God? Where did he and his descendants live? (Read Genesis 9:26 and Genesis 10:22-32).
    b. Where did Abraham live? (Read Genesis 11:31).

---

[1] K. Ham, M. Oard, *The New Answers Book 1,* Master Books. 2006, Chapter 16.

[2] A. A. Snelling and Mike Matthews, *When Was the Ice Age in Biblical History?* April 1, 2013, <answersingenesis.org>.

Answers from the Bible

1. **Genesis 7:11-12, 18-19:** "In the six hundredth year of Noah's life, in the second month, the seventeenth day of the month, on that day all the fountains of the great deep were broken up, and the windows of heaven were opened. **12** And the rain was on the earth forty days and forty nights. **18** The waters prevailed and greatly increased on the earth, and the ark moved about on the surface of the waters. **19** And the waters prevailed exceedingly on the earth, and all the high hills under the whole heaven were covered."

2. **Ezekiel 14:14:** "'Even if these three men, Noah, Daniel, and Job, were in it, they would deliver only themselves by their righteousness,' says the LORD God."
   Hebrews 11:7: "By faith Noah, being divinely warned of things not yet seen, moved with godly fear, prepared an ark for the saving of his household, by which he condemned the world and became heir of the righteousness which is according to faith."
   2 Peter 2:5: "... and did not spare the ancient world, but saved Noah, one of eight people, a preacher of righteousness, bringing in the flood on the world of the ungodly,"

3. **Genesis 9:11-13:** "Thus I establish My covenant with you: Never again shall all flesh be cut off by the waters of the flood; never again shall there be a flood to destroy the earth." **12** And God said: "This is the sign of the covenant which I make between Me and you, and every living creature that is with you, for perpetual generations: **13** I set My rainbow in the cloud, and it shall be for the sign of the covenant between Me and the earth."

4. **Luke 3:23-37:** The genealogy of Jesus includes Shem and Abraham.

4a. **Genesis 9:26:** "And he said: 'Blessed be the LORD, The God of Shem, and may Canaan be his servant.'"
   Genesis 10: 22-32: Sephar and Mesha was most likely in South Arabia.[1]

4b. **Genesis 11:31:** "And Terah took his son Abram and his grandson Lot, the son of Haran, and his daughter-in-law Sarai, his son Abram's wife, and they went out with them from Ur of the Chaldeans to go to the land of Canaan; and they came to Haran and dwelt there." (The land or city of Ur was most likely in northern Arabia or modern day Iraq[2]).

---

[1] Bible Hub, <bibleatlas.org/sephar.htm>, accessed July 2015.

[2] Bible Hub, <bibleatlas.org/ur.htm>, accessed July 2015.

3.6 Science of Order, Energy and Beauty

No one can deny the existence of order, energy and beauty in our world. Order and life are inseparable. Previous discussions already pointed out the importance of unchanging laws of physics and the fine-tuning of the universe. Energy is also crucial for life, but utterly destructive if not contained. The world is wrapped in beauty – beauty that cannot possibly arise out of random unplanned chaos. Even some modern art that strikes the viewer as random conveys the intentional message of the artist. Order, energy and beauty therefore have one thing in common, and that is purpose.

• Order

Whether we like it or not, order surrounds us in our societies and in nature. Order, unlike random chaos, protects not only our moral and physical wellbeing, but also the existence of life itself. To keep order in any society, there needs to be laws and law enforcers.

Social animals living in groups or colonies, such as mongooses, wild dogs, bees and even ants, have strict rules to maintain order that is necessary for the survival of the colony. The Preamble, the introduction to the United States Constitution, explains the need for instituting laws as follows, "We the People of the United States, in Order to form a more perfect Union, establish Justice, insure domestic Tranquility, provide for the common defense, promote the general Welfare, and secure the Blessings of Liberty to ourselves and our Posterity, do ordain and establish this Constitution for the United States of America." However, the initial and ultimate Lawgiver is God himself.

The authors of the Bible recorded many laws given by God. There are three kinds of Biblical laws: moral, ceremonial and civil.[1] The distinction is man-made, and helps to understand their different purposes.

- Ceremonial laws: Ceremonial laws gave instructions on regaining right standing with God, remembrances of God's work, specific regulations meant to distinguish Israelites from their pagan neighbors, and signs that pointed to the coming Messiah.
- Civil laws: These included laws regarding issues such as restitution for damage and the responsibility of a neighbor to help with a trapped donkey. In our world, this will include laws regarding speed limits, curfews, building codes and more.
- Moral laws: Moral laws are eternal and universal, and provide moral and ethical boundaries across all nations. God summarized it in the 10 Commandments to

[1] *What is the difference between the ceremonial law, the moral law, and the judicial law in the Old Testament?* <gotquestions.org/ceremonial-law.html>, accessed August 2015.

include regulations on justice, respect and sexual conduct. It is the absolute standard for morality and a mirror to see our own sin and moral depravity. In the New Testament, Jesus raised the bar even higher when he gave the greatest commandment,[1] and said that your thoughts alone can make you guilty of immoral acts such as murder or adultery.[2] An impossible standard you may say, however, should we expect anything less from a perfect and righteous God?

Order also reigns in the non-living world. Nature reveals spectacular examples of order that arise under the right conditions merely from the inherent chemical properties of molecules. The basalt columns of Giant's Causeway in Northern Ireland (top right[3]) and the cuboidal crystals of iron pyrite or "fools' gold" (bottom right[3]) are great examples. Even the sun, a large ball of hydrogen plasma, demonstrates order in the complex motions and alignments of the granules and super granules.[4]

When scientists discovered how laws, like gravity, govern the universe in an orderly way, they assumed that they could write simple equations defining the way things work, and then successfully predict outcomes. However, they soon came upon "chaotic" exceptions, such as wobbles in planets' orbits, turbulence in the airflow patterns of a plane's wing or ripples in the sand, which could not be explained by their equations.[5] Upon deeper investigation, they discovered that there is in fact mathematical order in apparently chaotic systems. Thus the "chaos" theory was developed, which attempts to find predictability in otherwise unpredictable behavior.

"All chaotic systems seem to have an unusual sensitivity to initial conditions. They are systems in which seemingly inconsequential changes turn into major differences in outcome. Scientists have found evidence of 'chaos' in astronomy, epidemiology, meteorology, air turbulence, the stock market and the human body. It is in the study of the human body that some scientists are beginning to realize just

---

[1] Matthew 22:36-39

[2] Matthew 5

[3] Photo courtesy of Dr. M. Meintjes.

[4] Dr. J. Lisle, *New Discoveries of Order in the Sun Astronomy.* April 1, 2012, <answersingenesis.org/astronomy/sun/new-discoveries-of-order-in-the-sun>.

[5] M. Blakefield, *Order or Chaos?* June 1, 1998, <answersingenesis.org/evidence-for-creation/order-or-chaos>.

how important chaos is," writes Martha Blakefield.[4] It seems that "chaos" is not the right term after all, it is just that the mathematics to explain the patterns are more involved. This knowledge may greatly enhance scientists' ability to make predictions as in the case of weather forecasting.

The complex and fascinating order in shapes, patterns and chaos in the non-living world reflects the ordered nature of the Creator. The biological world also demonstrates an incredible yet vastly different kind of order. The smallest cell cannot exist without multifaceted specific instructions and order. Imagine a car manufacturing plant where workers add parts randomly when they feel like it. No one will expect the car to operate safely, if at all. The wheels may fly off at 60 mph or the brakes may fail. It is the stuff of nightmares.

It is important to understand this difference, because some evolutionists have suggested that "chaos physics" could explain how the universe created its own complexity. Mrs. Blakefield clarifies that,

> living things, on the other hand, are characterized by truly complex, information-bearing structures, whose properties are not intrinsic to the physics and chemistry of the substances of which they are constructed; they require the pre-programmed machinery of the cell. This programming has been passed on from the parent organisms, but had to arise from an intelligent mind originally, since natural processes do not write programs. Any suggestion that the two issues are truly analogous denies reality.[1]

In short, both the non-living and living world functions because of order. The order in the non-living world is a product of chemical properties and laws of chemistry and physics. The order required for life demands the addition of information and pre-determined purpose. And purpose can only be established and enforced by an intelligent being.

"For the LORD of hosts has purposed, and who will annul it? His hand is stretched out, and who will turn it back?" (Isaiah 14:27)

---

[1] M. Blakefield, *Order or Chaos?* June 1, 1998, <answersingenesis.org/evidence-for-creation/order-or-chaos>.

Your turn to dig deeper: Order

1. Did you know that God of the Old Testament is a God of order who also requires order? (Read Leviticus 24:8, 2 Samuel 23:5 and 1 Chronicles 15:13).

2. Is He still a God of order in the New Testament? (Read 1 Corinthians 14:33 and 40, 1 Corinthians 14:31-33 and 1 Corinthians 15:23).

3. God is unchanging, so His laws should not change. However, Christians do not keep all the laws of the Old Testament, such as sacrificing animals, avoiding pork and writing off debts every seventh year. Did God change His mind or are we not obeying His laws? Examine the three kinds of laws: ceremonial, civil and moral to answer this question.
   a. List some ceremonial laws as well as their purposes. What did they symbolize? Which ceremony do you think was the most important? (Read Leviticus 7:11, Leviticus 14, Leviticus 20:25-26, Numbers 15:8-9, 27-28 and 1 Corinthians 14:26-29).
   b. Did ceremonial laws change between the Old and the New Testament? If yes, then why? (Read Matthew 5:17, Mark 7:7-9, Romans 14:5, 1 Corinthians 10:28, Galatians 3:23-24 and Galatians 6:15).
   c. Why do we not sacrifice animals anymore? (Read Hebrews 9:12 and Ephesians 2:15-16).
   d. Civil laws: (Read Exodus 18:20-22). What are civil laws? Do our civil laws sometimes change? Is that acceptable?
   e. Moral laws: Read the 10 Commandments in Exodus 20:1-17 and Jesus' summary of the greatest commandment in Matthew 22:36-39. Did God change His moral laws? Compare the 10 Commandments and Leviticus 20:9-15 with Matthew 5:17-32 and Romans 1:26-31. May we change God's moral laws?[1]

4. The fourth commandment concerns the keeping of the Sabbath. (Read Exodus 20:9-10, Exodus 31:13). Most Christians worship on Sunday instead of Saturday (the Sabbath), because Jesus rose from the dead on Sunday. Is that acceptable? What did Jesus and later Paul say about the intent of keeping the Sabbath? (Read Matthew 12:1-8, John 7:23 and Colossians 2:16).

Answers from the Bible

1. **Leviticus 24:8:** "Every Sabbath he shall set it in order before the LORD continually, being taken from the children of Israel by an everlasting covenant."

---

[1] For and in-depth study of the 10 Commandments read, *God's Blueprint for Life, Liberty, & Property: A Bible Study on the Ten Commandments*, by Stephen McDowell.

2 Samuel 23:5: "Although my house is not so with God, yet He has made with me an everlasting covenant, ordered in all things and secure. For this is all my salvation and all my desire."

1 Chronicles 15:13: "For because you did not do it the first time, the LORD our God broke out against us, because we did not consult Him about the proper order."

2. **1 Corinthians 14:33 and 40:** "For God is not the author of confusion but of peace, as in all the churches of the saints. [40]Let all things be done decently and in order."

1 Corinthians 15:23: "But each one in his own order: Christ the first fruits, afterward those who are Christ's at His coming."

3a. **Leviticus 7:11:** "For the life of the flesh is in the blood, and I have given it to you upon the altar to make atonement for your souls; for it is the blood that makes atonement for the soul."

Leviticus 20:25-26: "You shall therefore distinguish between clean animals and unclean, between unclean birds and clean, and you shall not make yourselves abominable by beast or by bird, or by any kind of living thing that creeps on the ground, which I have separated from you as unclean. [26]And you shall be holy to Me, for I the LORD am holy, and have separated you from the peoples, that you should be Mine."

Numbers 15:27-28: "And if a person sins unintentionally, then he shall bring a female goat in its first year as a sin offering. [28]So the priest shall make atonement for the person who sins unintentionally, when he sins unintentionally before the LORD, to make atonement for him; and it shall be forgiven him."

3b. **Matthew 5:17:** "Do not think that I came to destroy the Law or the Prophets. I did not come to destroy but to fulfill."

Mark 7:7-9: "'And in vain they worship Me, teaching as doctrines the commandments of men.' [8]For laying aside the commandment of God, you hold the tradition of men —the washing of pitchers and cups, and many other such things you do.'" [9]He said to them, 'All too well you reject the commandment of God, that you may keep your tradition.'"

Romans 14:5: "One person esteems one day above another; another esteems every day alike. Let each be fully convinced in his own mind."

1 Corinthians 10:28: "But if anyone says to you, 'This was offered to idols,' do not eat it for the sake of the one who told you, and for conscience sake; for 'the earth is the Lord's, and all its fullness.'"

Galatians 3:23-24: "But before faith came, we were kept under guard by the law, kept for the faith which would afterward be revealed. [24]Therefore the law was our tutor to bring us to Christ, that we might be justified by faith."

Galatians 6:15: "For in Christ Jesus neither circumcision nor uncircumcision avails anything, but a new creation."

3c. **Hebrews 9:12:** "Not with the blood of goats and calves, but with His own blood He entered the Most Holy Place once for all, having obtained eternal redemption."

Ephesians 2:15-16: "... having abolished in His flesh the enmity, that is, the law of commandments contained in ordinances, so as to create in Himself one new man from the two, thus making peace, [16]and that He might reconcile them both to God in one body through the cross, thereby putting to death the enmity."

3d. **Exodus 18:20-22:** "And you shall teach them the statutes and the laws, and show them the way in which they must walk and the work they must do. [21]Moreover, you shall select from all the people able men, such as fear God, men of truth, hating covetousness; and place such over them to be rulers of thousands, rulers of hundreds, rulers of fifties, and rulers of tens. [22]And let them judge the people at all times. Then it will be that every great matter they shall bring to you, but every small matter they themselves shall judge. So it will be easier for you, for they will bear the burden with you."

3e. **Exodus 20:1-17** is one of the most important chapters in the Bible.

Matthew 22:36-39: "'Teacher, which is the great commandment in the law?' [37]Jesus said to him, 'You shall love the Lord your God with all your heart, with all your soul, and with all your mind.' [38]This is the first and great commandment. [39]And the second is like it: 'You shall love your neighbor as yourself.' [40]On these two commandments hang all the Law and the Prophets.'"

Leviticus 20:9-15 details penalties for breaking the law.

Romans 1:26-32 demonstrates God's wrath on unrighteousness.

4. **Exodus 20:9-10:** "Six days you shall labor and do all your work, [10]but the seventh day is a Sabbath of the LORD your God; in it you shall not do any work, you or your son or your daughter, your male or your female servant or your cattle or your sojourner who stays with you."

Exodus 31:13: "Speak also to the children of Israel, saying: 'Surely My Sabbaths you shall keep, for it is a sign between Me and you throughout your generations, that you may know that I am the LORD who sanctifies you.'"

Matthew 12:1-8 says Jesus is Lord of the Sabbath.

John 7:23: "If a man receives circumcision on the Sabbath, so that the law of Moses should not be broken, are you angry with Me because I made a man completely well on the Sabbath?"

Colossians 2:16: "So let no one judge you in food or in drink, or regarding a festival or a new moon or Sabbaths."

• Energy

Energy, something teenagers strangely lack when facing chores, is critical for biological life. We trace the source of this energy, as well as hydroelectric, solar and wind energy, back to the magnificent ball of nuclear energy up in the sky, about 92 million miles away. The constant fusion reactions of our star, the sun, radiate enough photons to sustain all the energy cycles on earth. The sun is special in many ways. For example, it is remarkably stable compared to other stars, and it is just the right size to make it uniquely suited to support life.

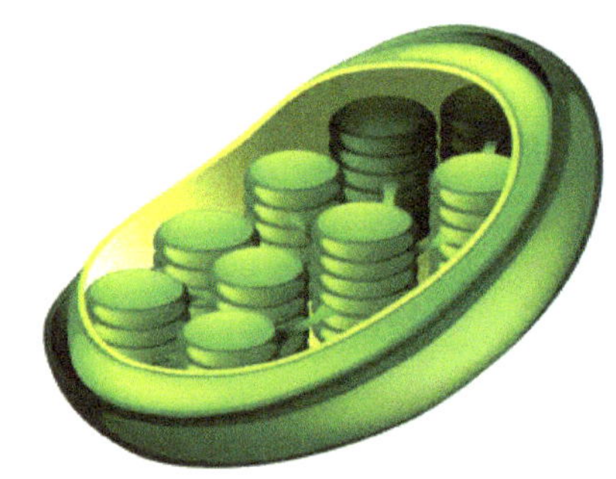

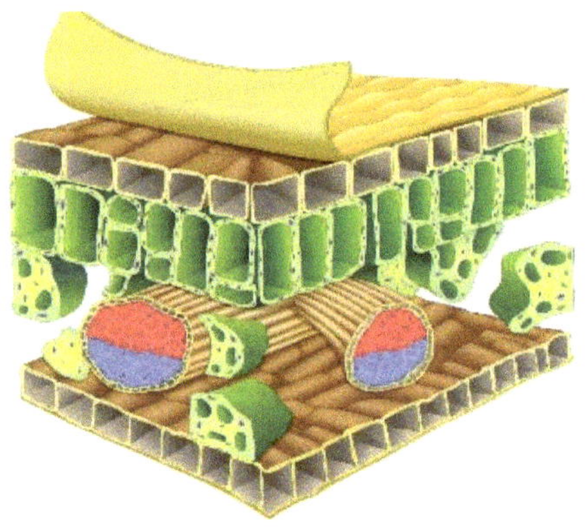

However, the sun would be useless if living cells could not utilize its energy. Random molecules can absorb energy from sunrays and vibrate faster all day long, but it can never convert solar energy into bio-available energy. For that, you need chloroplasts: complex housing systems, which contain the remarkable chlorophyll molecules. Chloroplasts are life's microscopic solar panels found in all green plants and algae. However, these chloroplasts cannot assemble or exist on their own.

Chloroplasts must be inside the protective environment of the fully functional cell. The cell must also provide the infrastructure to transfer and store the energy. The sticky issue is that a cell cannot assemble without a source of energy, and a source of energy cannot exist without a cell. This is one of the countless examples of irreducible complexity.

Irreducible complexity means that all parts must be functional and in place at the same time for successful operation. Space engineers who design and build spacecraft to send astronauts and satellites into space can write books about irreducible complexity. Their accomplishments are astounding. It is a testimony to the ability of the human mind, which itself also relies on order, energy and engineering marvels.

All life, from the bottom to the top of the food chain, is dependent on the irreducibly complex solar energy converters. To build them requires purpose, not to mention intricate coding and intelligence beyond our own. The biochemical pathways and nano-machines necessary to transfer, store and use the electricity generated by the solar panels, is yet another spectacular story.

To get an idea of some of these amazing nano-machines, watch an award-winning 3D-animation of the power converter stations called "mitochondria."[1] The clip shows how the mitochondria churn out adenosine triphosphate (ATP) molecules. If we think of the cell's energy units as "currency," then ATP molecules would be small "bills" of chemical energy derived from the breakdown of carbon-based food. ATP is a small complex and unstable molecule with a significant job. It acts as the fuel to power all the cellular machines. Errors anywhere along the intricate energy cycle, from photosynthesis to ATP production, often result in death or disease.

Next time you stare at a campfire and feel the heat of the dancing flames, consider that you are actually enjoying the sun's powerful nuclear energy from several years ago. Energy captured by tiny solar panels and stored within carbon bonds, while the tree stretched its branches towards heaven to bask in the sunshine.

Your turn to dig deeper: Energy

1. On what day did God create the sun and stars? How does He differentiate between them? (Read Genesis 1:14-19).
2. The sun radiates light and energy to sustain biological life. People love to bask in its rays and often feel depressed when there is a lack of sunlight. The human spirit also needs sunlight. Where can we get it? (Read Malachi 4:2 and John 8:12).
3. There is nothing random about the sun, moon and earth's unique ability to sustain life. The energy of the sun is constant. Earth is just the right distance away in an almost circular orbit. The tilt and rotation eliminate wide fluctuations in temperature. The moon reflects the sun's light and tugs at the oceans to keep them stirred up and healthy. Have you ever wondered what will happen if this fine energy balance is upset? For example, what if the earth's spinning slows down? The documentary, *What If the Earth Stops Spinning?*[2] gives an intriguing overview of this concept.
4. Does this delicate balance remain all by itself? (Read Hebrews 1:3 and Colossians 1:17).

---

[1] Harvard University and XVIVO, *The Mitochondria.* Biovision, <multimedia.mcb.harvard.edu>.

[2] *What if the Earth Stops Spinning (Full Documentary).* December 27, 2013, <youtube.com>.

Answers from the Bible

1. **Genesis. 1:14-19:** "Then God said, 'Let there be lights in the firmament of the heavens to divide the day from the night; and let them be for signs and seasons, and for days and years; [15]and let them be for lights in the firmament of the heavens to give light on the earth;'; and it was so. [16]Then God made two great lights: the greater light to rule the day, and the lesser light to rule the night. He made the stars also. [17]God set them in the firmament of the heavens to give light on the earth, [18]and to rule over the day and over the night, and to divide the light from the darkness. And God saw that it was good. [19]So the evening and the morning were the fourth day."

2. **Malachi 4:2:** "But to you who fear My name The Sun of Righteousness shall arise with healing in His wings ... "

   John 8:12: "Then Jesus spoke to them again, saying, 'I am the light of the world. He who follows Me shall not walk in darkness, but have the light of life.'"

4. **Hebrews 1:3:** "... who being the brightness of His glory and the express image of His person, and upholding all things by the word of His power, when He had by Himself purged our sins, sat down at the right hand of the Majesty on high ..."

   Colossians 1:17: "And He is before all things, and in Him all things consist."

• Beauty

Beauty flows from the physical properties of order and energy and is the result of purposeful creation. It may be one of the invisible attributes of God that Paul refers to in Romans 1:20. There is no survival benefit of beauty, and random mutations cannot explain its existence. Any computer programmer will appreciate the complex and additional coding required for elaborate patterns, shapes and colors.

Flowers, butterflies and feathered creatures are adourned with intricate designs and colors. The elegance and graceful movements of lions, cheetahs, antelopes and horses display exquisite beauty. We see beauty in the combination of colors in nature such as brilliant blue skies with white clouds racing across, or endless varieties of green grasses clinging to dark jagged rocks. We never tire of watching fiery sunsets, the beauty lingering until the orange ball drops from sight. The amazing thing is that the photoreceptor cells in our eyes are sensitive to "visible light," which lies in a very small region of the electromagnetic spectrum. It enables us to see our magnificent world in full color. However, beauty is not limited to sight alone.

The Continental Divide Trail in Colorado.[1]

We have ears that are tuned to pick up beauty in sound waves. Songbirds make some of the most beautiful music on earth. Apart from mating calls, there are no survival benefits for their carefully constructed cheerful songs. To produce a melody requires musical creativity and skill, selecting very particular notes with very specific timing. Some birds sing with different phrases that complement each other, and others even end their songs with an interval that signals the end of a song, such as a

---

[1] Photo courtesy of Dr. M. Meintjes.

major third or major fifth.[1] Musicians must study for years to master the skills that come naturally to birds.

It goes without saying that people and music are joined at the hip. Through our song, music and rhythm we express joy or sadness, and share our stories and messages. Undeniable is the fact that music has tremendous emotional impact for good or bad. It creates atmosphere, fills lonely hours, stimulate the intellect, and can make our spirits soar. It can also create fear and anxiety, and arouse physical desires. No one is immune to the emotional power of music. Unlike birds who have a preset, inbuilt musical tune with limited ability to mimic sounds, humans are exceptionally creative and purposeful in their art and musical expressions. No animal has this ability, not even a chimpanzee.

What a privilege it is to perceive beauty with all our senses. Wafting aromas of pine, cinnamon, leather, and roses are quick to trigger fond memories. Even better is the ability to enjoy the endless variety of scrumptious food and drinks, especially when accompanied by the laughter of friends. We often take the joy of touch for granted – a hug, a cozy blanket, cool refreshing air or water. The beauty that surrounds us on this stunning planet called Earth, reflects God's love for beauty. While nature glorifies God through displaying its splendor, God gave man senses to admire and enjoy the beauty, and a voice to give Him glory.

"You are worthy, O Lord to receive glory and honor and power;
For You created all things, and by Your will they exist and were created."
(Revelation 4:11)

---

[1] Prof. S. C. Burgess, *Beauty—The Undeniable Witness.* December 21, 2014, <answersingenesis.org>.

Your turn to dig deeper: Beauty

1. What is the role of music in the Bible? (Read 1 Samuel 16:23, 1 Chronicles 13:8, 2 Chronicles 20:21, Ecclesiastes 7:5, Acts 16:25-26 and 1 Corinthians. 15:51-52).
2. What does the Bible say about beauty? (Read Psalm 50:2, Psalm 149:4 and Matthew 6:28-29).
3. God made man in His image, but what kind of beauty is He looking for? (Read 1 Samuel 16:7, Proverbs 31:30 and 1 Peter 3:3-4).
4. Will there be beauty in heaven? (Read 1 Corinthians 2:9, Revelation 21:9-27).

Answers from the Bible

1. **1 Samuel 16:23:** "And so it was, whenever the spirit from God was upon Saul, that David would take a harp and play it with his hand. Then Saul would become refreshed and well, and the distressing spirit would depart from him."

   1 Chronicles 13:8: "Then David and all Israel played music before God with all their might, with singing, on harps, on stringed instruments, on tambourines, on cymbals, and with trumpets."

   2 Chronicles 20:21: "And when he had consulted with the people, he appointed those who should sing to the Lord, and who should praise the beauty of holiness, as they went out before the army and were saying: 'Praise the Lord, For His mercy endures forever.'"

   Ecclesiastes 7:5: "It is better to hear the rebuke of the wise than for a man to hear the song of fools."

   Acts 16:25-26: "But at midnight Paul and Silas were praying and singing hymns to God, and the prisoners were listening to them. [26]Suddenly there was a great earthquake, so that the foundations of the prison were shaken; and immediately all the doors were opened and everyone's chains were loosed."

   1 Corinthians 15:51-52: "Behold, I tell you a mystery: We shall not all sleep, but we shall all be changed— [52]in a moment, in the twinkling of an eye, at the last trumpet. For the trumpet will sound, and the dead will be raised incorruptible, and we shall be changed."

2. **Psalm 50:2:** "Out of Zion, the perfection of beauty, God will shine forth."

   Psalm 139:14: "I will praise You, for I am fearfully and wonderfully made; marvelous are Your works ... "

   Psalm 149:4: "For the LORD takes pleasure in His people; He will beautify the humble with salvation."

   Matthew 6:28-29: "So why do you worry about clothing? Consider the lilies of the field, how they grow: they neither toil nor spin; [29]and yet I say to you that even Solomon in all his glory was not arrayed like one of these."

3. **1 Samuel 16:7:** "But the LORD said to Samuel, 'Do not look at his appearance or at his physical stature, because I have refused him. For the LORD does not see as man sees; for man looks at the outward appearance, but the LORD looks at the heart.'"

   Proverbs 31:30: "Charm is deceitful and beauty is passing, but a woman who fears the LORD, she shall be praised."

   1 Peter 3:3-4: "Do not let your adornment be merely outward—arranging the hair, wearing gold, or putting on fine apparel— [4]rather let it be the hidden person of the heart, with the incorruptible beauty of a gentle and quiet spirit, which is very precious in the sight of God."

4. **1 Corinthians 2:9:** "But as it is written: 'Eye has not seen, nor ear heard, nor have entered into the heart of man the things which God has prepared for those who love Him.'"

   Revelation 21:9-27 describes the beauty of the New Jerusalem.

3.7 Science of Life

Having already discussed the order, complexity and beauty of life, there remains the task of attempting to clarify life itself. Since the word "life" has so many meanings, it is easy to mix up life puzzle pieces. Misconceptions and confusion regarding terms used in the study of life make matters worse.

To explain, let us imagine you are an astronaut who just found an amino acid (a building block of protein) on Mars. On Earth, the headlines will blast: "Astronaut found life on Mars!" Undoubtedly, that will go down as the biggest day of your life! A single cell has life, but some argue that the fetus in the womb does not. According to God, life ("nephesh" in Hebrew) is in the blood, and plants do not have life. Life seems to have many colors; in fact, the Merriam-Webster online dictionary gives 20 different meanings of the word "life." When discussing life, it is therefore extremely important to define which kind you are talking about. I would like to make a clear distinction between biological life and spirit life, and will discuss them separately.

• Biological Life – The First Cell

Textbooks define biological life as an ordered living unit able to grow, respond to stimuli, burn energy, maintain homeostasis and reproduce. These requirements are foundational for all living beings, whether it is a single cell organism or a human being. The enormity of this field compares to a limitless playground of discovery. No wonder people spend their lives studying the macroscopic, microscopic and molecular world of life. What they find is truly astounding.

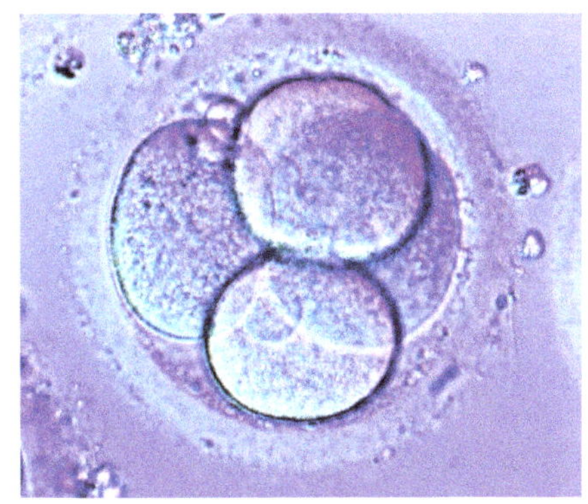

However, back in Darwin's day, scientists had no idea of the complexity of the cell, and therefore found the idea of spontaneous generation of life quite plausible. They considered cells featureless "bags of enzymes" with basic chemical reactions. (Photo on right is a 4-cell human embryo[1]) Findings from the fields of genetics, epigenetics, cell biology, molecular biology and biochemistry, have long since revealed the advanced technology of the cell. This begs a fundamental question: If a cell is so complex, where did the first one come from? Contrary to popular belief, the theory of evolution does not answer this question.

An analogy may be helpful to describe the conundrum of the first cell. Let us admire for a minute the technical genius, energy and order necessary to build and

---

[1] Photo courtesy of Dr. M. Meintjes.

operate a modern submarine, an impressive vessel that prowls the deep. Now, we take the thousands of parts, including computer processors, screens, hard drives, blueprints, fuel, metal plates, audio equipment, nuts, bolts, pipes, switches, nuclear reactor parts and dump them into the ocean. How long will it take the submarine to assemble itself? Perhaps some magnetic parts will cling to steel plates and electric cords can entangle other parts, but you can easily point out numerous reasons why the submarine will never assemble itself. Each of those reasons also apply to the auto-assembling of a single cell.

Just like the submarine parts, molecules have no inherent ability or tendency to assemble into more complex functional structures. As said before, it lacks information-bearing order. We stand humbled before the complexity of even the simplest single-cell organisms, like archaea; only now it dawns on us how little we know. To explain, let us look at the information required for nano-archaea, the tiniest known living cells, to function and replicate itself.[1] They have the smallest known genome (set of genes) with a mere 490,000 base pairs of DNA (Deoxyribonucleic acid, see page 69). This means that each tiny cell has an instruction book with 980,000 of the letters G, C, A and T. When typed out it would fill about 380 pages like this one! What an enormous amount of information packed into an organism 1/100 of the size of a tiny *Escherichia coli* bacterium. The inability of non-living molecules to assemble in an intelligent and purposeful way is not the only obstacle to spontaneous generation.

In 1952, Stanley Miller published his famous experiment claiming that amino acids, the building blocks of proteins, can form spontaneously in primordial soup. Primordial soup being the theoretical liquid on earth that gave rise to the first life. This experiment, however, was flawed. Unlike the situation in the real world, Miller isolated the sample liquid from the original heated source of "primordial soup." He had to, because heat and oxygen denature (destroy) amino acids as soon as they form. Furthermore, a few amino acids are a long way from complex 3D protein machines and blueprints necessary for life. The list of problems is endless. To this date, no secular scientist has solved the mystery of the first cell.

Since the theory of spontaneous generation has lately been rolling like a tumbleweed, many scientists are rethinking an old theory called "panspermia." In 1908, Arrhenius coined the name "panspermia" for the idea that life originated in outer space and then migrated to earth.[2] Some suggested that life precursors came on the back of meteors, but the heat and impact would have been devastating. More favorable is the belief that aliens seeded the first cells and evolution did the

---

[1] T. Niederberger, *Archaea – Prokaryote.* <britannica.com/science/archaea>, accessed October 2015.

[2] G. Purdom, *Did Life Come from Outer Space?* June 27, 2014, <answersingenesis.org/origin-of-life/panspermia/did-life-come-from-outer-space>.

rest. This is part of the reason why billions of dollars are spent looking for life in outer space. It is mostly about man's desire to understand his origin.

Actually, the source of life is from outer space, and the Bible documents who He is and how He did it. God not only created the earth and made it suitable for life, He also spoke all kinds of fully functional living creatures into existence. Amongst others, the word "alien" means, "Relating to or denoting beings supposedly from other worlds; extraterrestrial." (Oxford dictionary) In that sense, you can find many aliens in the Bible. Extraterrestrials (angels) often materialized. Some were messengers, others received power to fight wars, blind men and destroy cities.[1] Those, who serve in the Throne Room, have four faces, those of a man, lion, ox and eagle, the figure and hands of men, the feet of calves and four wings![2]

Just because our biological senses cannot detect God's other-dimensional world, it does not mean it is a fanciful tale. Nonetheless, the part of God's creation that we can see clearly reflects His divine power and intelligence. The more our technology advances, the more we can admire this.

• Biological Life – The First Cell of New Life

Especially fascinating is the miracle of every new human life, which starts out as an oocyte, the largest cell in the body. (Photo on right[3]) She is the "queen" of all cells, and here is her story:

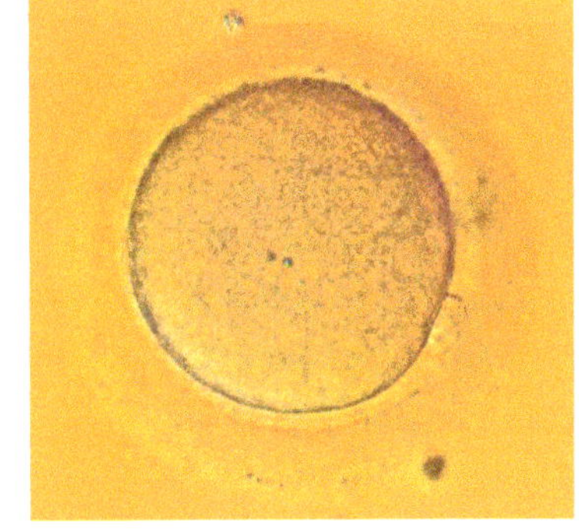

Exactly on time, the queen exits her chamber and travels regally down the red carpet laid out for her. The most important meeting of her life awaits. She carries not only half of the blueprint for life (in the form of 23 chromosomes), but she also has all the battery packs, power plants, supplies and equipment needed for the next few critical days.

Hours later, the first of millions of tiny suitors (sperm) surround her. Each suitor carries the other half of the chromosomes and even two fishing rods (centrosomes)! For them, it is a desperate journey because there can be only one winner. A thick coat (zona pellucida) protects the queen. Slowly but surely, the suitors tunnel their way into the coating using cutting tools (enzymes). The moment the first one breaks through, the queen raises a firewall, sealing off the losers.

Magically, it seems, the two half sets of chromosomes drift towards the center of the cell and pair up. (Actually, they are steered by complex motor proteins and microtubules). A myriad of machinery descends on the 46 chromosomes to unroll,

---

[1] Luke 1, 26-38, Genesis 19, 11 Kings 6

[2] Ezekiel 1

[3] A human oocyte wrapped in the zona pellucida. Photo courtesy of Dr. M. Meintjes.

unzip and replicate gigabytes of information stored on the almost 3 billion units (base pairs of DNA) at breakneck speed. The most amazing dance of information exchange between the pairs of chromosomes follows to give the baby unique characteristics. During this organized mayhem, the queen became an embryo, the priceless beginning of new life.

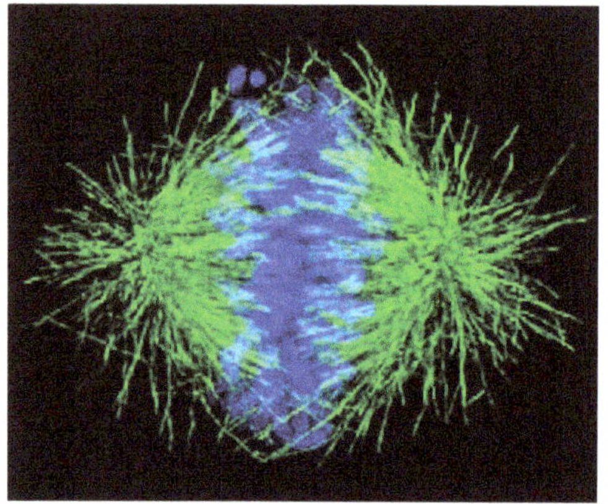

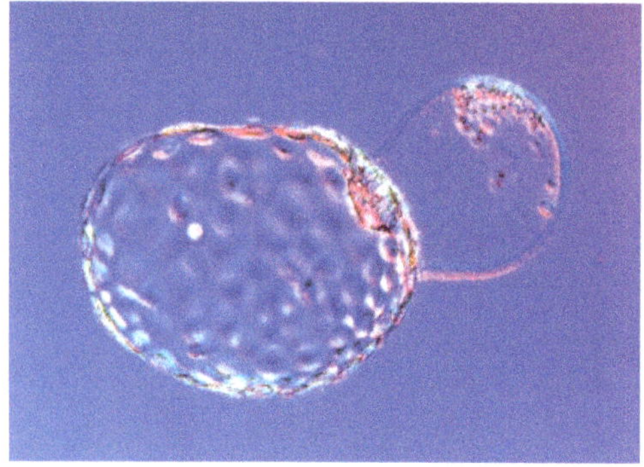

Shortly after, two identical sets of complete blueprints neatly line up in the middle of the cell. Meanwhile, the two fishing rods (centrosomes with spindles) move to the opposite ends of the cell and go to work. They each cast multiple lines (microtubules) to catch the chromosomes from opposite sides. (The photo top left shows mitotic spindles, green, and chromosomes, blue.[1]) Once all the lines are secure, the one-cell embryo is ready to divide in two. The fishing rods reel the chromosomes in and the cell membrane divides, completing the first cell division.

Over the next few days, the cells divide about every 12 hours. By the sixth day, the embryo must "hatch" from the protective layer. (The photo bottom left shows the beginning of hatching in a human embryo.[2]) At this point, some of the cells have become the future baby and others have become the life capsule (placenta). By now, the fuel demand has increased tremendously. It is time to link up the tiny being's shelter to a new lifeline, the womb, where the next amazing phase of the journey awaits.

"For You formed my inward parts; You covered me in my mother's womb. I will praise You, for I am fearfully and wonderfully made; Marvelous are Your works, and that my soul knows very well. My frame was not hidden from You, when I was made in secret, and skillfully wrought in the lowest parts of the earth. Your eyes saw my substance, being yet unformed. And in Your book they all were written, the days fashioned for me, when as yet there were none of them."

(Psalm 139:13-16)

---

[1] Photo courtesy of Dr. L. Pelletier. <lunenfeld.ca/about-us/discovery-corner-stories/dr-laurence-pelletier-and-his-research-team-use-breakthrough-technology-to-visualize-cell-division-in-unprecedented-detail>.

[2] Photo courtesy of Dr. M. Meintjes.

Your turn to dig deeper: Biological Life - The First Cell

1. Genesis 1 describes how God created life. Note that "life/living" refers to the soul ("nephesh" in Hebrew), which is the domain for consciousness, memories, emotions and instincts. More on this topic in the chapter, "Man's Nature."
   a. Do plants have life? (Read Genesis 1:11-12).
   b. Do fish, birds and other animals have life? (Read Genesis 1:20-24).

2. The Bible further clarifies life (nephesh) in an interesting manner. (Read Leviticus 17:11). What do you think it means? The first cells of the embryo receive oxygen and nutrients by diffusion. As the embryo grows exponentially, the metabolic demands increase at the same rate. Therefore, the cardiovascular system is the first to develop. Actual blood flow can already be seen by the end of 21 days;[1] around the time a woman realizes she may be pregnant. What implications does this have on the beginning of life or the "personhood" of an embryo?

3. Upon clinical death, all biochemical and electrical activity have ceased. It is an irreversible finality. However, there is someone greater than the physical and chemical laws governing biological life. (Read John 11:1-40).
   a. How long did Jesus delay His visit?
   b. Why?
   c. What had already happened to Lazarus' body?
   d. How many times does the Bible refer to resurrection of the dead? Which one is the most important? An article summarizing these resurrections, *Raise the Dead,* is available online at <stronginfaith.org/article.php?page=114>.

---

[1] S. T. Blackburn, *Maternal, Fetal, & Neonatal Physiology: A Clinical Perspective.* 3rd Edition, Elsevier Health Sciences. *2007,* 287.

Answers from the Bible

1a. **Genesis 1:11-12:** "Then God said, 'Let the earth bring forth grass, the herb that yields seed, and the fruit tree that yields fruit according to its kind, whose seed is in itself, on the earth;' and it was so. [12]And the earth brought forth grass, the herb that yields seed according to its kind, and the tree that yields fruit, whose seed is in itself according to its kind. And God saw that it was good."

1b. **Genesis 1:20-24:** "Then God said, 'Let the waters abound with an abundance of living creatures, and let birds fly above the earth across the face of the firmament of the heavens.' [21]So God created great sea creatures and every living thing that moves, with which the waters abounded, according to their kind, and every winged bird according to its kind. And God saw that it was good. [22]And God blessed them, saying, 'Be fruitful and multiply, and fill the waters in the seas, and let birds multiply on the earth.' [23]So the evening and the morning were the fifth day. [24]Then God said, 'Let the earth bring forth the living creature according to its kind: cattle and creeping thing and beast of the earth, each according to its kind;' and it was so."

2. **Leviticus 17:11**: "For the life of the flesh is in the blood, and I have given it to you upon the altar to make atonement for your souls; for it is the blood that makes atonement for the soul."

3. **John 11:1-40** tells of Lazarus rising from the dead.

• Evolution, Mutation, and Adaptation

At this point, it may be a good idea to clarify the theory of evolution and related terms. According to the Merriam-Webster Dictionary, evolution is "a theory that the differences between modern plants and animals are because of changes that happened by a natural process over a very long time." While Darwin never claimed to answer the question of the origin of life, people just assumed that the same natural random processes built the first cells. From thereon, cells added beneficial information to their genetic code via random changes. With an information system open to random changes, cells somehow managed to determine when informational gain was beneficial, and then saved those changes for future generations. Cells also gained new instructions incrementally to, perhaps, grow a tail and later to make it move. Scientists claim that beneficial mutation is the biological mechanism for the incremental changes.

Mutation is defined as "the changing of the structure of a gene, resulting in a variant form that may be transmitted to subsequent generations, caused by the alteration of single base units in DNA, or the deletion, insertion or rearrangement of larger sections of genes or chromosomes."[1] Depending on the location, the smallest mutation may result in horrendous suffering or death. One such painful and fatal disease is junctional epidermolysis bullosa. It robs a baby from speech and sight and scars his body inside and out, just because he is missing a protein that binds layers of skin.

The concepts of "vestigial organs" and "junk DNA" as mutation remnants from our ape ancestor days, have become very popular in support of the theory of evolution. In 1893, a German anatomist named Robert Wiederheim, published a list of 86 useless organs, such as the vermiform appendix, Os coccyges and Cauda humana. Today we know the functions of just about all these organs. For example, the appendix acts as a crucial storage space for beneficial bacteria. Scientists are also beginning to unravel the complex role of "junk DNA." The ENCODE group recently produced a "stunning inventory of previously hidden switches, signals and sign posts embedded like runes throughout the entire length of human DNA."[2]

The model of beneficial mutation as the mechanism for evolutionary changes has significant limitations. For instance, there are no examples of beneficial mutation, not even sickle cell anemia or bacterial resistance, because mutations are always detrimental to the overall survival of the species.[3] Also, mutation can only alter pre-existing DNA. Even though mutation can result in new traits, such as

---

[1] Merriam-Webster Dictionary

[2] S.S. Hall, *Hidden Treasures in Junk DNA*. <scientificamerican.com/article/hidden-treasures-in-junk-dna/>, October 1, 2012.

[3] *Beneficial mutations: real or imaginary*? Video clip available at <creation.com/media-center>.

wingless beetles, it does not add new information. Some use the concept of beneficial mutation synonymously with the term "microevolution."

Microevolution is the "evolutionary change within a species or small group of organisms, especially over a short period."[1] This implies a gain of genetic information to account for differences within same kinds, even though no one has ever been able to demonstrate a gain of new information. Scientists have grown bacteria through thousands upon thousands of replication cycles while doing research. They may find minor trait variances within the populations, but round bacteria (cocci) remains round bacteria, rods remain rods and spiral bacteria will remain spiral bacteria. Unless you use your intelligence and do some genetic engineering, you will never get a different kind of creature. Micro-evolution is a misnomer. How then is it possible that we still observe new species formation?

A "species" is "a group of living organisms consisting of similar individuals capable of exchanging genes or interbreeding." "Speciation" is defined as "the formation of new and distinct species in the course of evolution."[1] Speciation is one of the main arguments evolutionists use to support evolution. However, genetic variation (of existing genetic make-up) through the process of adaptation or natural selection, is normal and observable in offspring. This enables animals spread out over different areas to adapt and flourish in their respective environments. Speciation requires that the differences become so great between varieties that they cannot interbreed anymore, hence the birth of a new species. Examples include hawthorn flies, greenish warblers and Croatian lizards. Molecular biologists now suspect that retro-elements (jumping genes) play a critical role in mammalian speciation.[2]

The point of this brief discussion on speciation is this: Since none of the available speciation examples demonstrates a change in kind, speciation has nothing in common with evolution as the definition claims. Flies are still flies, finches are still finches, warblers are still warblers and the lizards are still lizards.

When Darwin visited the Galapagos Islands, he observed not evolution, nor micro-evolution, but finch adaptation or natural selection. This is "a change, or the process of change, by which an organism or species becomes better suited to its environment."[3] We see this often in one-cell organisms, but also in plants and animals. Bacterial resistance to antibiotics is an example.

Bacteria, unlike plants and animals, have an amazing ability to mutate and exchange genetic information amongst members of the colony. Harmless strains of bacteria can degenerate into destructive infectious organisms via loss of genetic

---

[1] Oxford Dictionary

[2] P. Jerlström, *Jumping wallaby genes and post-Flood speciation.* <creation.com/jumping-wallaby-genes-and-post-flood-speciation>, accessed November 2015.

[3] Merriam-Webster Dictionary

information, plasmid acquisition, and/or gene translocation.[1] There is never a gain of new genetic information. While using an antibiotic, some bacteria may lose the enzymes to "digest" the antibiotic. As a result, the antibiotic cannot kill these bacteria; therefore, they as well as subsequent generations become resistant "superbugs." These bacterial colonies, however, retain only a subset of the original code. They have lost genetic diversity and adaptability to other environments in the process. This makes them more vulnerable overall. Loss of genetic diversity is a one-way street to extinction.

All plants, animals and even humans have a genetic ability to adapt because God created the first plants, animals and humans with the complete set of information to code for variation to ensure survival. Isolated populations that inbreed eventually lose genetic diversity and become disease-ridden, infertile and extinct. All wildlife managers, animal breeders and veterinarians guard against the disastrous effects of inbreeding and subsequent loss of genetic diversity. Furthermore, instead of an ever-improving human genome, we see degeneration as genetic errors accumulate with each subsequent generation. This problem worsens in a small genetic pool, such as the case of the "Royal Disease," which cropped up in the children of Queen Victoria. They could not understand why so many of the royal family members suffered excessive bleeding, a recessive gene disorder that we know today as hemophilia.[2]

Adolf Hitler once said that if you tell a big enough lie and you tell it frequently enough, people will eventually believe it. He was right. Years of repetition and media headlines have made the unproven theory of evolution, mainstream ideology in science. To go against it, is to hit a wall. I urge you, dear reader, to diligently search for truth. Remember that science has limits, and that scientists are merely fallible human beings. Believing that God created all life according to their kind during the Creation week, is not a prerequisite to go to heaven. But, know that you are treading on an extremely dangerous and slippery slope when you trust man's word and opinions above those of God.

Your turn to dig deeper: Evolution, Mutation and Adaptation

1. The Bible did not use Linnaeus' classification system, but rather listed plants and animals according to kinds who cannot interbreed. What kinds of plants and animals did God create in Genesis 1?

---

[1] A. Gillen, F. Sherwin, *The origin of bubonic plague*. Journal of Creation 20 (1):7-8 April 2006. Also available at <creation.com>.

[2] Y. Aronova-Tiuntseva, C. Feeman, *Hemophilia" "the Royal Disease.* <sciencecases.lib.buffalo.edu/cs/files/hemo.pdf>, accessed October 2015.

2. In what order did God create the plants and animals? Does it match the evolution theory's order?

3. One of the most commonly asked questions is, "Where did Cain, Adam and Eve's first son, find a wife?" (Read Genesis 4:17). Can you figure it out? (Read Acts 17:26, Genesis 3:20, 4:1 and 5:4). Remember that only important events of those first few hundreds of years were recorded.

4. Regarding marriage between close relatives:
   a. Who was Abraham's wife? (Read Genesis 20:11-12).
   b. What laws did God institute about 400 years after Abraham's time? (Read Deuteronomy 27:22 and Leviticus 18).
   c. Why do you think God gave these laws? Consider relational issues and accumulations of mistakes in genetic material. Read the article referenced below for further study on the topic.[1]

Answers from the Bible

1. **Genesis 1** details the history of creation.

3. **Genesis 4:17:** "And Cain knew his wife, and she conceived and bore Enoch ..."
   Acts 17:26: "And He has made from one blood every nation of men to dwell on all the face of the earth, and has determined their pre-appointed times and the boundaries of their dwellings."
   Genesis 3:20: "And Adam called his wife's name Eve, because she was the mother of all living."
   Genesis 4:1: "'Now Adam knew Eve his wife, and she conceived and bore Cain, and said, 'I have acquired a man from the LORD.'"
   Genesis 5:4: "After he begot Seth, the days of Adam were eight hundred years; and he had sons and daughters."

4a. **Genesis 20:11–12:** "And Abraham said, 'Because I thought, surely the fear of God is not in this place; and they will kill me on account of my wife. But indeed she is truly my sister. She is the daughter of my father, but not the daughter of my mother; and she became my wife.'"

4b. **Deuteronomy 27:22:** "'Cursed is the one who lies with his sister, the daughter of his father or the daughter of his mother.' And all the people shall say, 'Amen!'"
   Leviticus 18 clarifies the laws of sexual morality.

---

[1] <compellingtruth.org/relationship-close-relative.html>
<answersingenesis.org/contradictions-in-the-bible/too-close-for-comfort>

• Information and Communication

Our age is called the "information age," not because we are intellectually superior to previous generations, but because computers, smart phones and countless other digital devices have brought mountains of information to our fingertips. Technology has come a long way since the first telegraph message, and we get all excited over the sleek designs and smooth performances of our electronic gadgets. Yet, we quickly trash them when they quit communicating information. Just like our electronic communication equipment, each living cell must be able to safely store information and communicate it instantly upon demand.

The strange thing is, you can delete 64 GB of data from your smartphone and it will weigh the same. Well, that is somewhat stating the obvious, since information is nonmaterial. It has no physical properties and is separate from mass and energy. You cannot weigh it like flour, yet it is more powerful than any material entity in existence. Even so, the nonmaterial information needs a material medium for storage, use and display.

The most complex information on earth is stored, not on some mega computer built by man, but in the tiniest computer inside every nucleated cell of your body. The hard drive consists of strands of DNA – (deoxyribonucleic acid), which are tightly wound, twisted ladders of nucleotides. This 3D hard drive, the blueprint of life, repairs itself with complex nano-machines,[1] duplicates itself, opens and closes pages, and tells copier machines where to start and stop. Unlike our computer coding systems such as Java and C++, DNA uses four codes, "A," "T," "C" and "G" to convey the vast amounts of information required for life. Through the study of epigenetics, scientists have even found important commas and periods that are critical in the expression and transcription of the information. If you uncoil each strand of the DNA of all the trillions of cells in your body and line them up end to end, it will be billions of miles long.[2]

Just like computers and smart phones, a hard drive alone is not enough. To read and communicate the information, the cell uses a wide variety of intricate molecular machines that function at unbelievable speeds. XVIVO created excellent 3D animation videos of cellular functions. The clip, "The Inner Life of the Cell," gives an exciting glimpse into the operations of these fascinating little machines that keep you alive.[3] Many DVDs, such as "Unlocking the Mysteries of Life,"[4] vividly portray the bigger picture of the world of the cell, as far as scientists understand it today.

---

[1] *The Cells' Toolbox for DNA Repair*. Press release, 7 October 2015. <nobelprize.org>.

[2] C. Toledo and K. Saltsman, *Genetics by the Numbers*. June 11, 2012, <publications.nigms.nih.gov/insidelifescience/genetics-numbers.html>.

[3] *The Inner Life of The Cell*. <xvivo.net/animation/the-inner-life-of-the-cell>.

[4] *Unlocking the Mystery of Life, The Scientific Case for Intelligent Design*. DVD by Illustra Media.

Communication is not limited to the boundaries of the cell. All multi-cellular organisms need extra layers of communication between cells,[1] between the various organs of the body, and between the body and the brain. Think courier services, computer networks and trillions of internet connections. The brain, which controls this complex machine, is completely dependent on communication systems to receive feedback regarding the life support status and to execute commands.

My close encounters with majestic creatures and fascinating critters while growing up in South Africa left a permanent impression on me. My veterinary studies began to open my eyes to the many marvels of biological engineering on the macro and micro level. Did you know you use millions of molecular-sized springs inside your inner ear to hear? Dr. David Menton writes,

> the wiggling of the hairs causes small molecular 'trapdoors' on the tips of the hairs to open and close, permitting electrically charged particles (ions) to enter the hairs. Incredibly, the molecular trapdoors are controlled by molecular springs that attach to adjustable molecular brackets. It staggers the mind to think of tiny molecular trapdoors opening and closing at a rate between 20 and 20,000 times per second, admitting charged ions into the tips of the hairs.[2]

All creatures display an intricate design and advanced technology that require enormous amounts of information and communication systems.[3] Destin Sandlin, a rocket engineer, marvels at this often in his "Smarter Every Day" educational YouTube videos. For example, in his *Mantis Murder Shrimp* video, he explores the fascinating physics behind the Mantis Shrimp's deadly punch. Definitely worth watching.

Can you spot the lowly stick bug clinging to the mesquite leaves in the photo to the left? Nifty camouflage. The wonders of design are not limited to individual creatures, but also include complex systems of camouflage, co-dependence, imitations and attractions, both sweet and fatal.

Ever since man has discovered the superb technology in nature, he applied the information to improve his own technology.

---

[1] New research on the role of extracellular RNA communication, see video at <xvivo.net/animation/unlocking-the-mysteries-of-extracellular-rna-communication>.

[2] Dr. D. Menton, *The Hearing Ear*. August 29, 2007, <answersingenesis.org/human-body/the-hearing-ear>.

[3] For more information read Dr. J. Sarfatti's book, *By Design. Evidence for Nature's Intelligent Designer, the God of the Bible.* Creation Book Publishers. 2008.

For example, since the beginning of human flight, aviation engineers have examined birds to improve aircraft flight and performance. They still do today.[1] They snatch at parts of the technology, as they cannot yet understand or imitate the whole package. Fish scales inspired improvements in swimwear and body armor, squids led to the creation of "Robosquid," a self-propelled pulsed jet. Gecko feet help robots climb vertical.[2] Engineers at BAE Systems used the design of the eyes of the tiny parasitic fly to improve night vision goggles for frontline troops.[3]

Derek Muller also produces excellent science videos that are available on his YouTube channel, Veritasium. One in particular, *How to Make Colour With Holes,*[4] relates to this subject. The video commentary reads, "Scientists are being inspired by nature [in this case, butterfly wings] to design the next generation of security devices... Arrays of nanoscale holes create beautiful reflected colors that are almost impossible to forge. Soon these nanoscale security devices could replace holograms." This new technology is truly impressive; however, it still does not measure up to the complexity and design of the butterfly and its utterly amazing lifecycle.

With so many useful discoveries and applications of designs found in nature, a new discipline called "biomimicry" has emerged. Some universities, like Arizona State University, even offer degrees in this field. It will always be wise, most beneficial and exciting to learn from the Master Designer of the universe.

"Great are the works of the Lord; they are studied by all who delight in them."
(Proverbs 2:6, NASB)

Your turn to dig deeper: Information and Communication

1. God not only incorporated information and communication systems within biological life, but He also created living creatures with the ability to communicate.
   a. What does the Bible say about hearing? (Read Proverbs 20:12).
   b. Does God hear us? (Read Psalms 34:15 and Psalms 94:9).

---

[1] K. Reals, *Aircraft engineers look to bird world for new and improved wing designs*. August 9,2010, <flightglobal.com/news/articles/aircraft-engineers-look-to-bird-world-for-new-and-im-345832/>.

[2] For more detail read Ray Comfort and Jeffrey Seto's book, *Made in Heaven. Man's Indiscriminate Stealing of God's Amazing Design*. Master Books. 2012.

[3] <www.defense-aerospace.com/articles-view/release/3/107866/new-%E2%80%98bug-eye%E2%80%99-night-vision-kit-from-bae.html>

[4] Derek Muller, *How to Make Colour With Holes.* Jan 21, 2013, <youtube.com>.

2. In what ways did God communicate with people in Biblical times?
   a. Ever since his first encounter with God at the burning bush, Moses enjoyed God's presence in a special way. It even made his face shine at times. How did God communicate with Moses? (Read Exodus 3:4-6 and Exodus 33:11).
   b. During the conversations, could Moses see God's face in all His glory? (Read Exodus 33:20-23).
   c. How did God communicate with the great prophet Elijah? (Read 1 Kings 19:11-13).
   d. How did Jesus talk with Saul, who later became Paul, the first missionary? (Read Acts 9:3-6). Did the conversation change Paul? (Read Acts 9:20-22).

3. God does not often communicate audibly today as He did in Biblical times. Still, many Christians testify that God met them in a miraculous way and changed their lives.
   a. How does God commonly speak to us today? (Read John 16:12-13, 2 Timothy 3:16–17 and Romans 12:2).
   b. What did God say about adding to His prophecies in Revelations 22:18-19? Is John referring to the whole Bible or just Revelations?

Answers from the Bible

1a. **Proverbs 20:12**: "The hearing ear and the seeing eye, the LORD has made them both."

1b. **Psalms 34:15:** "The eyes of the LORD are on the righteous, and His ears are open to their cry."

Psalms 94:9: "He that planted the ear, shall he not hear? He that formed the eye, shall he not see?"

2a. **Exodus 3:4-6:** "So when the LORD saw that he turned aside to look, God called to him from the midst of the bush and said, 'Moses, Moses!' And he said, 'Here I am.' [5]Then He said, 'Do not draw near this place. Take your sandals off your feet, for the place where you stand is holy ground.' [6]Moreover He said, 'I am the God of your father—the God of Abraham, the God of Isaac, and the God of Jacob.' And Moses hid his face, for he was afraid to look upon God."

Exodus 33:11: "So the LORD spoke to Moses face to face, as a man speaks to his friend ..."

2b. **Exodus 33:20-23:** "But He said, 'You cannot see My face; for no man shall see Me, and live.' [21]And the LORD said, 'Here is a place by Me, and you shall stand on the rock. [22]So it shall be, while My glory passes by, that I will put you in the cleft of the rock, and will cover you with My hand while I pass by. [23]Then I will take away My hand, and you shall see My back; but My face shall not be seen.'"

2c. **1 Kings 19:11-13:** "Then He said, 'Go out, and stand on the mountain before the LORD.' And behold, the LORD passed by, and a great and strong wind tore into the mountains and broke the rocks in pieces before the LORD, but the LORD was not in the wind; and after the wind an earthquake, but the LORD was not in the earthquake; [12]and after the earthquake a fire, but the LORD was not in the fire; and after the fire a still small voice. [13]So it was, when Elijah heard it, that he wrapped his face in his mantle and went out and stood in the entrance of the cave. Suddenly a voice came to him, and said, 'What are you doing here, Elijah?'"

2d. **Acts 9:3-6:** "As he journeyed he came near Damascus, and suddenly a light shone around him from heaven. [4]Then he fell to the ground, and heard a voice saying to him, 'Saul, Saul, why are you persecuting Me?' [5]And he said, 'Who are You, Lord?' Then the Lord said, 'I am Jesus, whom you are persecuting. It is hard for you to kick against the goads.' [6]So he, trembling and astonished, said, 'Lord, what do You want me to do?' Then the Lord said to him, 'Arise and go into the city, and you will be told what you must do.'"

Acts 9:20-22: "Immediately he preached the Christ in the synagogues, that He is the Son of God. [21]Then all who heard were amazed, and said, 'Is this not he who destroyed those who called on this name in Jerusalem, and has come here for that purpose, so that he might bring them bound to the chief priests?' [22]But Saul increased all the more in strength, and confounded the Jews who dwelt in Damascus, proving that this Jesus is the Christ."

3a. **John 16:12-13**: "I still have many things to say to you, but you cannot bear them now. [13]However, when He, the Spirit of truth, has come, He will guide you into all truth; for He will not speak on His own authority, but whatever He hears He will speak; and He will tell you things to come."

2 Timothy 3:16–17: "All Scripture is given by inspiration of God, and is profitable for doctrine, for reproof, for correction, for instruction in righteousness, [17]that the man of God may be complete, thoroughly equipped for every good work."

Romans 12:2: "And do not be conformed to this world, but be transformed by the renewing of your mind, that you may prove what is that good and acceptable and perfect will of God."

3b. **Revelation 22: 18-19:** "For I testify to everyone who hears the words of the prophecy of this book: If anyone adds to these things, God will add to him the plagues that are written in this book; [19]and if anyone takes away from the words of the book of this prophecy, God shall take away his part from the Book of Life, from the holy city, and from the things which are written in this book."

• Evolution and Gospel Puzzle Pieces

There is another critical aspect to consider regarding the evolution puzzle piece before concluding the science section. In short, the two key puzzle pieces, evolution and the gospel, are so radically opposing that they will never fit on the same puzzle.

In an attempt to understand suffering in this world, Darwin became convinced that God does not care. His years of contemplation and his inquisitive mind led him to formulate his grandfather's ideas into the theory of evolution. The theory of evolution explains that man evolved from spiritless ape-men in the midst of disease, death and survival of the fittest. Since the molecules-to-man process is void of anything spiritual, man remains unrestrained by moral laws. He establishes his rule, serving only his survival instincts and physical pleasures. Evolution demands struggle, disease and death before perfection, which is the yet unattained but ultimate goal.

In contrast, Genesis 1 explains that God created everything "very good." This negates the idea of struggle, disease and death. On day six, he created Adam and Eve in His own image. After all, they were the reason He created the universe! He created them intelligent and creative, with the ability to love. He gave them purpose and wrote the moral laws in their hearts. When they disobeyed God, physical and spiritual death, as well as suffering entered the world. However, God did not abandon Adam and Eve. He promised to send a Savior, which He did.

Apostle Paul summarizes this good news, the gospel, as follows, "Therefore, as through one man's offense judgment came to all men, resulting in condemnation, even so through one Man's righteous act the free gift came to all men, resulting in justification of life." (Romans 5:18) But, how can the righteous and loving God, allow so much evil and suffering? The answer to this difficult question, which sadly eluded Darwin, is found in God's perfect love. The elimination of evil and suffering demands the destruction of sin. To destroy all sin, God must destroy all sinners, meaning all of us. In His infinite wisdom, He allows the evil and suffering to give more sinners the chance to repent, to accept His free gift and choose to love Him freely. The gospel is ultimately the good news of God's incredible love. (Read also Chapter 4:2 and 5.3)

If you choose to add evolution to your puzzle, the gospel cannot fit. Neither would the pieces about the rest of the Creation week when God created plants before the sun and marine life, birds before dinosaurs and all animals according to their kinds. Also off the table go Adam and Eve's children, the worldwide flood and everything supernatural. Examples include Enoch, who never died, the 10 plagues in Egypt, the parting of the sea, extended daylight, a talking donkey, Jesus' virgin birth, His miracles and resurrection, Phillip's instant transportation, Paul's conversion and the end times prophesies, to name a few. You will find that there is not much left of the Bible – which is exactly the point of the evolutionists.

Still, theologians have tried to find the missing link between evolution science and the creation week. They argue that God could have created life through the process of evolution. Enter the "theistic evolution" puzzle piece. Recently, someone commented that the term "theistic evolution" is an oxymoron. Theism claims God's mercy towards sinners who cannot save themselves, and evolution claims that man saved himself. Theistic evolution makes God an add-on to man's science and a liar. This puzzle piece will not fit anywhere. You are stuck with a choice between the evolution and gospel pieces.

Science has opened our eyes to the magnificence of our universe and the incomprehensible complexity of life. The question then is not IF there is a God, but rather WHO God is. I agree with C.S. Lewis, who wrote, "I believe in Christianity as I believe that the sun has risen. Not only because I see it, but because by it I see everything else."[1]

"I have made the earth, and created man on it. I—My hands—stretched out the heavens, and all their host I have commanded." (Isaiah 45:12)

Your turn to dig deeper: Evolution and Gospel Puzzle Pieces

1. If Adam was not a literal person, who in Genesis 5 do you accept as literal?
2. Read Romans 5:12-19. Why is it important to accept the fact that there was a literal Adam? Why does Adam carry the blame for the separation of all of mankind from God?
3. Evolution explains suffering, death and disease as a natural part of survival of the fittest. Yet, when disaster strikes, people quickly raise their fists at God. If He is a loving God, how could He allow it? In the midst of suffering and despair, this is a difficult question to answer. Why do we live in a broken world? (Read Genesis 3:17 and Romans 8:22).
4. What should our attitude be towards suffering unrelated to our own sin? (Read Romans 5:3-4, 2 Corinthians 4:17-18 and 1 Peter 4:12-14).

---

[1] C.S. Lewis, *They Asked For A Paper*, in *Is Theology Poetry?* London: Geoffrey Bless, 1962, 164-165.

Answers from the Bible

1. **Genesis 5** details Adam's family.

2. **Romans 5:12-19** demonstrates death through Adam, but life in Christ.

3. **Genesis 3:17:** "Then to Adam He said, 'Because you have heeded the voice of your wife, and have eaten from the tree of which I commanded you, saying, 'You shall not eat of it': Cursed is the ground for your sake; In toil you shall eat of it all the days of your life.'"

   Romans 8:22: "For we know that the whole creation groans and labors with birth pangs together until now."

4. **Romans 5:3-4:** "And not only that, but we also glory in tribulations, knowing that tribulation produces perseverance; [4]and perseverance, character; and character, hope."

   2 Corinthians 4:17-18: "For our light and momentary troubles are achieving for us an eternal glory that far outweighs them all. [18]So we fix our eyes not on what is seen, but on what is unseen, since what is seen is temporary, but what is unseen is eternal."

   1 Peter 4:12-14: "Beloved, do not think it strange concerning the fiery trial which is to try you, as though some strange thing happened to you; [13]but rejoice to the extent that you partake of Christ's sufferings, that when His glory is revealed, you may also be glad with exceeding joy. [14]If you are reproached for the name of Christ, blessed are you, for the Spirit of glory and of God rests upon you. On their part He is blasphemed, but on your part He is glorified."

Chapter 4
Man's Corner

Your skull is home to three pounds of the most complex matter in the universe. It stores terabytes of memories, emotions, sounds, smells and knowledge. It monitors a constant stream of input from trillions of sensors and directs energy, defense, repair and locomotion systems while connected to your soul and spirit. No wonder it is difficult to understand yourself, let alone anyone else. Humans are complex beings, which demand countless pieces for this corner of the puzzle. Though every human being is unique, we sail in the same boat when it comes to our nature, predicament and needs.

4.1 Man's Nature

In Mary Shelley's book *Frankenstein*, the doctor created a hideous, but overall good man in his lab, who turned into a very bad guy when everyone rejected him. Are people by nature good, bad or in between? Many believe that man is inherently good, like Frankenstein's monster. They think people only act badly because of unfair and hurtful treatment. While physical and emotional abuse maims lives like trampled flowers, this is about something else. The belief that man is inherently good cultivates self-righteousness, entitlement, and the justification of bitterness and revenge in response to hurt. It is difficult to admit and face your own faults if you believe you are inherently good. If we are honest with ourselves, I think we can agree man is not the picture of "moral goodness gone bad."

Aggression and selfishness seems woven into mankind's fabric. Evolutionists claim that this is a product of survival instincts. "The human failing I would most like to correct is aggression. It may have had survival advantage in caveman days, to get more food, territory or partner with whom to reproduce, but now it threatens to destroy us all," Dr. Stephen Hawking recently commented.[1] If man's nature is merely the product of instincts, there can be no blame for immoral acts. Furthermore, you have to trash the "meaning of life" puzzle piece. Harvard University paleontologist George Simpson claims that, "Man is the result of a purposeless and natural process that did not have him in mind."[2] Richard Dawkins explains in his book, *The Selfish Gene*, that you are just an accident who will never

---

[1] <blog.sciencemuseum.org.uk/insight/2015/02/20>, accessed August 2015.

[2] C. Raymo, *Skeptics and True Believers.* New York, NY: Walker. 1998, 345.

act for the good of your species. Your only purpose is to propagate your selfish gene. One man said he did not sleep for three nights after reading *The Selfish Gene*. He felt that his life had become empty and the universe no longer had a point.[1]

Our behavior often reflects that of animals, not because we evolved from them, but because we are totally self-absorbed by nature. Out of our dark hearts sputters pride, aggression, selfishness and the everlasting desire for pleasures. We find ourselves broken in an evil world, trying to understand why. It may be helpful at this point to examine man's nature through God's eyes.

God created us in His image as a triune being.[2] Each of us lives inside our physical body that will eventually return to dust. We also have a soul ("nephesh" in Hebrew, refers to "life" or "living") and spirit ("ruwach" in Hebrew, means "God's breath"). At first glance, it appears that the Bible uses the words "soul" and "spirit" interchangeably, but they are not the same. Paul wrote, "Now may the God of peace Himself sanctify you entirely; and may your spirit and soul and body be preserved complete, without blame at the coming of our Lord Jesus Christ." (1 Thessalonians 5:23)

Dr. Clarence Larkin, an influential Baptist pastor and author, depicted this threefold nature of man with an illustration of three circles. The outer circle represents the body, the middle circle the soul and the inner circle the spirit.[3]

- Outer circle - body: The five senses of touch, hearing, sight, smell and taste are the windows to man's body, connecting him to the physical world. The body in turn joins to the soul.
- Middle circle - soul: The soul is the domain for man's conscience, memory, reason and emotions. (Perhaps the measurable energy field of the body is part of the soul in some way.) The body and soul, in turn, connect the physical world to the inner circle, the domain of the human spirit.
- Inner circle - spirit: Man's spirit is his inner sphere of God-consciousness and understanding. The spirit enables faith, hope, reverence, prayer and worship. Our spirit will return to God when we die (Ecclesiastes 12:7).

The first sin closed Adam and Eve's windows to their "spirit chambers" to render utter darkness (more on this in the next section). Every human heart stays that way until the Holy Spirit enters this chamber with life-giving light, regenerating the old and giving new life in Jesus Christ. Almost like plugging a lamp into the electrical outlet and turning it on.

Contrary to man's explanations, God said you are a moral and spiritual being. In His eyes, you are beautiful, creative, intelligent and certainly NOT an accident. He

---

[1] Quoted from Bass, Thomas. *Interview* Omni, 1990, 12(4):60.

[2] <bible.org/seriespage/2-man-trinity-spirit-soul-body>, accessed August 2015.

[3] C. Larkin, *Rightly Dividing the Word of Truth.* Chart 22, <earnestlycontendingforthefaith.com>, accessed August 2015.

knew you before your birth, and He has loved you all the way. He cannot tolerate sin, but He is able to look beyond it and see you.

> *"Do you thus deal with the LORD, o foolish and unwise people? Is He not your Father, who bought you? Has He not made you and established you?"*
> *(Deuteronomy 32:6)*

Your turn to dig deeper: Man's Nature

1. What does it mean to be God's image bearer? (Read Genesis 1:26, 27 and 31). What are man's moral, spiritual, creative, intelligent and relational abilities?
2. Genesis 2:7 summerizes Adam's birth. Remember, "life/living creatures" refers to the soul (*nephesh*), and "breath" to the spirit (*ruwach*).
   a. What did God use to make Adam's body? Does the human body really consist out of elements from the earth?
   b. How did God give him a spirit?
   c. How does the verse describe Adam's soul?
3. Animals have emotion, appetites and intelligence, so they have a soul. Do they also have a spirit that gives them understanding? Will animals go to heaven? (Read Job 12:9-10, Job 32:8 and Psalm 32:9).
4. How did the people refer to God in Numbers 16:22?
5. What does the Bible say about the soul and emotions? (Read Genesis 34:8, 1 Samuel 18:1 and Proverbs 25:25).
6. While separated from God, is man by nature good, or evil? (Read Genesis 6:5, Psalm 51:5, Jeremiah 17:19 and Romans 3:23).

Answers from the Bible

1. **Genesis 1:26, 27 and 31:** "Then God said, 'Let Us make man in Our image, according to Our likeness; let them have dominion over the fish of the sea, over the birds of the air, and over the cattle, over all the earth and over every creeping thing that creeps on the earth.' 27So God created man in His own image; in the image of God He created him; male and female He created them. 31Then God saw everything that He had made, and indeed it was very good. So the evening and the morning were the sixth day."
2. **Genesis 2:7:** (KJV) "And the LORD God formed man of the dust of the ground, and breathed into his nostrils the breath of life; and man became a living soul."

3. **Job 12:9-10:** "Who among all these does not know that the hand of the LORD has done this, [10]In whose hand is the life of every living thing, and the breath of all mankind?"
   Job 32:8: "But there is a spirit in man, and the breath of the Almighty gives him understanding."
   Psalm 32:9: "Do not be like the horse or the mule, which has no understanding..."

4. **Numbers 16:22:** "Then they fell on their faces, and said, 'O God, the God of the spirits of all flesh, shall one man sin, and You be angry with all the congregation?'"

5. **Genesis 34:8:** "But Hamor spoke with them, saying, 'The soul of my son Shechem longs for your daughter. Please give her to him as a wife.'"
   1 Samuel 18:1: "Now when he had finished speaking to Saul, the soul of Jonathan was knit to the soul of David, and Jonathan loved him as his own soul."
   Proverbs 25:25: "As cold water to a weary soul, so is good news from a far country."

6. **Genesis 6:5:** "Then the LORD saw that the wickedness of man was great in the earth, and that every intent of the thoughts of his heart was only evil continually."
   Psalm 51:5: "Behold, I was brought forth in iniquity, and in sin my mother conceived me."
   Jeremiah 17:9: "The heart is deceitful above all things, and desperately wicked; who can know it?"
   Romans 3:23: "For all have sinned and fall short of the glory of God."

4.2 Man's Predicament

During those first days, Adam and Eve lived in an exquisite garden, loaded with delicious foods ready for the picking. During the cool of the evenings, their Creator walked and talked with them. He was wealthy, intelligent, loving and wise beyond imagination. They never feared Him; they had no reason to. They were ignorant of evil, surrounded only by good.

In the middle of the Garden, God had planted two trees. The Tree of Life represented His way of life and wisdom. From this tree, Adam and Eve could eat their fill. The other tree, the Tree of Knowledge of Good and Evil, represented man's wisdom apart from God and the way of death. God clearly forbid Adam and Eve to eat from this tree, warning that death would follow if they did. Because the tree offered a choice, it represented the potential, but not the existence of evil.

Good is fundamental and can exist in itself, however, evil, which is a parasite on good, cannot. It would be the same for a wound, which presupposes the existence of a healthy body, explains Dr. Sarfati.[1] God declared seven times that His creation was "good" and "very good" in Genesis 1. There was no evil in the beginning when God created Adam and Eve. But in the midst of the beauty and perfect goodness, something went wrong, terribly wrong.

It started when Satan confronted Eve at the Tree of Knowledge of Good and Evil. With a cleverly crafted question and a half-truth,[2] Satan undermined God's character. Eve was quick to follow his line of thinking. She realized God has been holding out on them ... how could He? "So when the woman saw that the tree was good for food, that it was pleasant to the eyes and desirable to make one wise, she took of its fruit and ate. She also gave to her husband with her, and he ate." (Genesis 3:6) In his insightful book, *Good or God?*, John Bevere points out that Eve was not attracted to anything bad; on the contrary, she only saw "good." What, then, did Eve do wrong?

Eve's first mistake was to doubt God's wisdom, goodness and righteousness. Once she decided she knew better, she found it easy to disobey God's command. Eve could make this choice because God gave her, Adam and the angels the "power of contrary choice," which is the ability to make a choice that goes against their good nature.[1] This choice was good in itself because it enabled people to choose to love God freely. After all, only love given freely is genuine love.

---

[1] J. Sarfati, *Refuting Compromise.* Master Books. 2004, 197.

[2] Genesis 3:1-5

In that cataclysmic moment when both Adam and Eve ate the fruit, they rejected God's supreme authority. The Holy Spirit left their inner spirit chambers with a finality that echoed throughout the universe. A dark void, deprived of truth and light, remained. It was a state of spiritual death. In the darkness, they could not see God anymore. Their newfound knowledge of good and evil opened their eyes to their nakedness and guilt. Suddenly they were fearful[1] of the One who showered them with goodness and provided for all their needs.

Adam and Eve were fearful because of the way they perceived evil. God knew about evil the same way an oncologist (cancer specialist) knows about cancer. After Adam and Eve ate the fruit, they knew evil in the same way cancer sufferers know cancer, explains Pastor John MacArthur.[2] Adam, Eve and the rest of mankind lost their power of contrary choice and their good nature when they rejected God's authority over their lives. Separated from God, filled with fear and guilt, Adam and Eve could only act according to their sinful nature and corrupted bodies – a fate they passed on to the rest of humanity.

People can investigate, reason and make intelligent decisions regarding things of this world. They have worldly knowledge of good and evil, but are thoroughly confused about right and wrong as long as darkness reigns in their spirit chambers. That lonely, dark void prompts the never-ending desire to be filled. Like a submarine without sonar, man blindly searches for something to fill the void. It is a dire predicament indeed.

"And even as they did not like to retain God in their knowledge, God gave them over to a debased mind, to do those things which are not fitting; being filled with all unrighteousness, sexual immorality, wickedness, covetousness, maliciousness; full of envy, murder, strife, deceit, evil-mindedness; they are whisperers, backbiters, haters of God, violent, proud, boasters, inventors of evil things, disobedient to parents, undiscerning, untrustworthy, unloving, unforgiving, unmerciful; who, knowing the righteous judgment of God, that those who practice such things are deserving of death, not only do the same but also approve of those who practice them." (Romans 1:28-32)

---

[1] Genesis 3:10

[2] J. MacArthur, *The Battle for the Beginning.* Nashville, TN: W Publishing Group. 2001, 211.

Your turn to dig deeper: Man's Predicament

1. If God made Adam inherently good (Genesis 1), where did things go wrong?
   a. What did God command Adam to do in Genesis 2:17?
   b. What do you think God meant by the "knowledge of good and evil?"
   c. Did Adam obey God? (Read Genesis 3:6).

2. Genesis 3 gives the serpent credit for his craftiness. Can you spot his deception? (Read Genesis 3:1, 4 and 5).
3. List the reasons Eve gave to justify eating the forbidden fruit. (Read Genesis 3:6). Do people do the same today?
4. Adam and Eve's single action of disobedience irreversibly cracked and tainted the perfect world, both physically and spiritually. Do you fully understand the consequences? (Read Genesis 3:14-19).

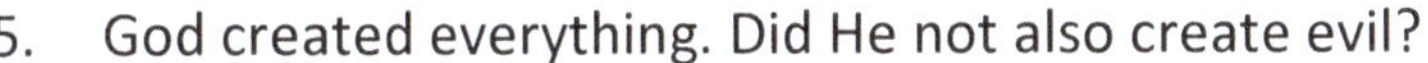

5. God created everything. Did He not also create evil?
   a. What is evil? Can evil be created?
   b. Is calamity or disaster the same as evil? Does God have the right to cause calamity? (Read Isaiah 45:7).
6. Can our dead and dormant spirits know or understand God? (Read Ephesians 2:1 and 1 Corinthians 2:14).

Answers from the Bible

1. **Genesis 2:17:** "... but of the tree of the knowledge of good and evil you shall not eat, for in the day that you eat of it you shall surely die."

2-4 **Genesis 3:1-19** details the temptation and fall of man.

5. **Isaiah 45:7:** "I form the light and create darkness, I make peace and create calamity; I, the LORD, do all these things."

6. **Ephesians 2:1:** "And you He made alive, who were dead in trespasses and sins."

   1 Corinthians 2:14: (NASB) "But a natural man does not accept the things of the Spirit of God, for they are foolishness to him; and he cannot understand them, because they are spiritually appraised.

4.3 Man's Needs

In our consumer-driven society, we drink from a fire hose of advertisements about things we "need." They deceptively blur the lines between wants and needs. In reality, we have wants and needs unique to our body, soul and spirit. It makes sense, then, to look at each part individually.

I think of the body as a marvelous planetary suit, complete with the ability to grow, convert energy, repair and defend itself. It comes equipped with climate control and an array of sophisticated sensors. These controls and sensors are technologically advanced far beyond anything man can build. In all, NASA's $12 million space suits[1] cannot even begin to compare. Just think – you got yours for free!

Unlike man-made engines and devices, the suit can endure an amazing amount of neglect and dirty fuel before breaking down. For obvious reasons, people must take care of their suit. Some needs are critical, but most time and money are generally spent decorating and enhancing the suit. Mankind is seriously preoccupied with outward appearances. Therefore, they easily forget that while the suit is useful to identify them, it certainly does not define who they are. It is merely a biological vessel of their soul and spirit during their brief journey on Earth.

It is important to recognize that sin corrupted not just the soul, but also the suit. The suit seems to have a mind of its own and is determined to run the show. Unless there is a prospect of something more desirable, the suit resists exertion of any kind. It prefers pleasing things: beds, couches, sugar and an endless list of actions that release brain-tickling hormones such as dopamine and endorphins. Synthetic stimulants, of course, are much more desirable (the suit gets an intensely desirable kick out of those). The suit does not care much about the consequences until it is too late. Since the suit does not have digital displays to indicate fuel-, oil- and coolant levels, it communicates needs and wants with what we experience as cravings or desires.

Signs of hunger, thirst, fatigue and temperature extremes are easy to signal, but vitamin, micronutrient or mineral shortages are not so easy. These sometimes show up as weird cravings. The suit will quickly send food back up the tube if it detects certain toxins. Other toxins, however, enter the bloodstream leaving the filter systems to clean them up ... up to a point. Years of dumping drugs, alcohol, food additives and loads of nutrient-empty, processed food down the hatch, will eventually take its toll on the suit. It will seize up, leaving the soul and spirit stuck on the side of the road. Since you get only one of these suits in your lifetime, it is wise

---

[1] C. C. Freudenrich, *How Space Suits Work.* <science.howstuffworks.com>, accessed September 2015.

to take proper care of it. Rest, exercise and a healthy, natural diet will go a long way towards optimal performance.

The body-soul connection provides another reason to take care of your suit. For example, chronic pain or disease often leads to depression or despair. Alcohol and drugs fry your brain cells, clouding your decisions and feelings. It works the other way around as well. Negative emotions like bitterness can cause physical diseases. Anxiety may lead to increased blood pressure and an impaired immune system. A growing body of evidence now links depression to an increase risk for osteoporosis where bones become brittle and fracture easily. King Solomon understood this when he wrote in Proverbs 22:17 that a joyful heart is like good medicine, but that a broken spirit dries up the bones. The body-soul interaction is complex, affecting us in more ways than we realize.

The soul is the seat for your memories, reason and affections. It is who you are. It is the essence of your personality, and you came pre-wired with a unique one. Even identical twins have different personalities. With your unique personality, you received wonderful talents and gifts. Every human soul longs for acceptance, security and significance. Anyone who has been without human contact for some period, or who has suffered intense emotional loss, will be able to tell you about the powerful impact of a caring hug.

The soul, bent and vulnerable as the result of sin, is the place where Satan appeals to your emotions and desires. Remember, he is the great Deceiver, a master at cloaking death and destruction as something "good" and "desirable." His tactics worked exceptionally well with Eve, and he has no doubt improved them since then. Satan whispers that one can fill the void with "good" things, such as your own big self and just a little more gold, glory and girls/guys. He offers the world's endless excitement and pleasures on a plate. He especially serves up the kinds of pleasures that slowly erode the mind and body.

Satan tirelessly works to destroy human life, but his ultimate goal is to enter the void in the inner spirit chamber and take control. He is not free to enter because man's will guards the door... most of the time. Satan has many ways to deceive people into dropping their guards. For example, if he can lure a person into participating in occult rituals, even if it is just for "fun," and surrender control of his mind, the door may just crack open wide enough for Satan or some of his minions to slip in. The Bible calls it demon possession.[1]

Initially, the Deceiver does an expert job providing excitement and entertainment. Someone observed that Satan has a lot of happy young people, but no happy old people. Eventually, most find that the pleasures are short lived, and

---

[1] Matthew 8, 9, 12, 15, 1 Corinthians 10:20 and 1 Timothy 4:1

the price too high. They realize that Satan has lied. Worshipping themselves does not fill the void. Some tire of the ugliness and self-loathing that follow on the heels of dirty pleasures. They yearn to become new and clean – for a fresh start. Perhaps they go to counselors or try "12 steps to recovery." They promise tomorrow will be different. Never again.

At some point though, it dawns on them that they have utterly failed at fixing themselves. With the Holy Spirit gently prodding their souls, they finally face the blackness in their soul and spirit and realize their dire need to be guilt free. Perhaps now they are ready to consider God, whose unconditional love is bigger than life itself. It is at this place of brokenness that God does His greatest work of redemption.

At this point, man faces the most important decision of his life. Since God never forces man to love and obey Him, man has to willingly open the door of his spirit chamber in full submission to Jesus as Lord and King. Only then will the Holy Spirit enter with His divine light and truth! He creates a new man, forgiven, washed as white as snow. Angels rejoice when God puts the pieces of a broken life back together to make it beautiful. God's perfect love fuels the changes necessary to love Him back. His grace, which is unmerited favor, not only saves them, but also empowers them to walk in His steps.

With His power, they gain victory over foul thoughts, foul deeds and foul chemicals. With eyes that now can see and a mind that understands, they finally taste real happiness, true joy and peace of mind. God alone fulfills their deepest need for love, acceptance, security and significance. He does it in royal abundance.

"But as it is written: 'Eye has not seen, nor ear heard, nor have entered into the heart of man the things which God has prepared for those who love Him.' But God has revealed them to us through His Spirit. For the Spirit searches all things, yes, the deep things of God. For what man knows the things of a man except the spirit of the man which is in him? Even so no one knows the things of God except the Spirit of God." (1 Corinthians 2:9-11)

Your turn to dig deeper: Man's Needs

1. Can we determine what is good? (Read Proverbs 14:12).
2. What happens if we cling to our own way of life? (Read Romans 2:5).
3. What does the Bible say about the human body and spirit? (Read Romans 8:5 and Galatians 5:17).
4. How does Paul compare the importance of the body to the soul? (Read 1 Timothy 4:8).

5. What did Jesus say about demon posession? (Mark 9:25-29, Luke 11:24-26).

6. Satan tried to tempt Jesus by offering to fulfill Jesus' needs. (Matthew 4:1-11).
   a. What needs did Satan address?
   b. Why? How did Jesus respond?
   c. Who served Him in the end?

7. Who can take care of all your needs? (Read Philippians 4:19).

Answers from the Bible

1. **Proverbs 14:12:** "There is a way that seems right to a man, but its end is the way of death."

2. **Romans 2:5:** (NSAB) "But because of your stubbornness and unrepentant heart you are storing up wrath for yourself in the day of wrath and revelation of the righteous judgment of God."

3. **Romans 8:5:** "For those who live according to the flesh set their minds on the things of the flesh, but those who live according to the Spirit, the things of the Spirit."
   Galatians 5:17: "For the flesh lusts against the Spirit, and the Spirit against the flesh; and these are contrary to one another, so that you do not do the things that you wish."

4. **1 Timothy 4:8:** "For bodily exercise profits a little, but godliness is profitable for all things, having promise of the life that now is and of that which is to come."

5. In **Mark 9:25-29,** Jesus cast out the deaf and dumb spirit.
   Luke 11:24-26: "When an unclean spirit goes out of a man, he goes through dry places, seeking rest; and finding none, he says, 'I will return to my house from which I came.' **25**And when he comes, he finds it swept and put in order. **26**Then he goes and takes with him seven other spirits more wicked than himself, and they enter and dwell there; and the last state of that man is worse than the first."

6. In **Matthew 4:1-11,** Satan tempts Jesus.

7. **Philippians 4:19:** "And my God shall supply all your needs according to His riches in glory by Christ Jesus."

Chapter 5

The LORD God

A pastor once said that your idea of who God is compares to the top button of your shirt. If it is off, everything else in your life will be off! For many, the idea of who God is comes from who they want God to be. Others claim you cannot really know who He is. God asks, "To whom then will you liken Me, or to whom shall I be equal?" (Isaiah 40:25) Can you answer? Let us look at three key puzzle pieces for this final, but most important corner of the Life Puzzle: God's greatness, His holy nature and His perfect love.

5.1 God's Greatness

Professor Robert Wilson taught at Princeton Theological Seminary during the early 1900s. One day, he listened to a sermon by Dr. Donald Barnhouse, a former student who returned to campus as a guest preacher. After the sermon, Professor Wilson told Dr. Barnhouse that he came to listen for only one reason: he needed to know whether his student was a "big God-er" or a "little God-er." He referred to the belief regarding the greatness of God.

There are many little God-ers in this world, who believe in a limited god. Some believe that the Christian God is a mystical being, like the ancient Greek god Zeus, the god of thunder. Dr. Lennox explains it this way: Assume for a second you wholeheartedly believe in Zeus. Well, you will have a nasty surprise waiting when you enter Atmospheric Physics 101. Zeus does not cause thunder and lightning after all. It is the result of temperature gradients, static electricity and vibrations through the atmosphere ... exit your god![1] If you define your god as only a placeholder for the unexplainable in the physical realm, then you serve a small god indeed! Many scientists also have this misconception about God.

They assert that the more they learn about the universe, the less likely the existence of God is.[2] An analogy may help to test this statement. Suppose someone studied a beautiful house extensively and then proclaims, "I have studied the flooring, the rooms, the structure, the materials used and the layout, and I cannot find the architect anywhere! So clearly, he is a myth!" What an absurd argument. This, however, is exactly the kind of argument some scientists use. We can find the architect everywhere, because the house is his handiwork. He is not the laws that

---

[1] J. Lennox, *Science and Faith,* 2013 Pensmore Dialogue.

[2] *Will Science Someday Rule Out the Possibility of God?* <livescience.com/23251-science-religion-god-physics.html>, accessed July 2015.

the house operates by, or the building material, but He is the designer and builder. Hebrews 3:4 states, "For every house is built by someone, but He who built all things is God." Scientific discovery does not diminish God. It greatly exalts Him! King David wrote, "The heavens declare the glory of God; and the firmament shows His handiwork. Day unto day utters speech, and night unto night reveals knowledge. There is no speech nor language where their voice is not heard." (Psalm 19:1-3)

It is natural to wonder where God came from. Philosophers call it the ultimate cause problem: If God created the universe, then who created God, and what created whatever created God? This is a complex question, meaning it hides assumptions. In this case, it hides the assumption that God was actually created. If God was not created, this question no longer applies. The apostle John wrote, "All things were made through Him, and without Him nothing was made that was made." (John 1:3) What a profound statement! If you ask who created God, you are assuming that God came to be. John claims that without Him, nothing was made that was made. God is responsible for His own existence. How can it be? We cannot wrap our finite minds around the greatness of God.

The Bible clearly declares God's omnipotence, transcendence, magnificence and righteousness. "'Am I a God near at hand,' says the LORD, 'And not a God afar off? Can anyone hide himself in secret places, so I shall not see him?' says the LORD; 'Do I not fill heaven and earth?' says the LORD." (Jeremiah 23:23-24) King David wrote, "O God, You are my God; I shall seek You earnestly; My soul thirsts for You, my flesh yearns for You, in a dry and weary land where there is no water. Thus I have seen You in the sanctuary, to see Your power and Your glory." (Psalm 63:1-2, NASB)

Joshua, Caleb and 10 other spies returned to report on everything they saw in the Promised Land.[1] They reported that the land overflowed with milk and honey, but that the people were powerful giants. The 10 spies were terrified because they compared the giants to themselves. However, Joshua and Caleb compared the giants to their God and were fearless. They were big God-ers and lived a life of victory! It turns out that Dr. Barnhouse was also a big God-er. He became an acclaimed minister, author and a radio pioneer, who influenced countless lives and glorified his King. His faith was big, because his God is big.

"Thus says the LORD: 'Heaven is My throne, and earth is My footstool. Where is the house that you will build Me? And where is the place of My rest? For all those things My hand has made, and all those things exist,' says the LORD. 'But on this one will I look: On him who is poor and of a contrite spirit, and who trembles at My word.'" (Isaiah 66:1-2)

---

[1] Numbers 13

Your turn to dig deeper: God's Greatness

1. Do you think that Jehovah God could have created the incalculable universe? (Read Psalm 90:2, Isaiah 40:28, Jeremiah 32:27, Daniel 4:35, Matthew 19:26 and Revelation 21:6).
2. The author of Hebrews asked, "What is mankind that you are mindful of them, a son of man that you care for him?" (Hebrews 2:5-7)
   a. If God is so great, aren't people too small in His eyes? (Read Deuteronomy 7:9, Jeremiah 23:23-24 and Psalm 103).
   b. Did you know that you are about halfway between the size of our solar system and a proton? (Visit *The Scale of the Universe,* <htwins.net/scale2>).
3. Name three differences between God and man listed in Numbers 23:19.
4. Since God is all-powerful, His name is powerful. Therefore, people foolishly use it to add power to their statements. Nevertheless, God's name is holy. (Read Exodus 20:7).
   a. What does it mean to use God's name in vain?
   b. Will you dare to use God's name in vain if you understand who He really is?

'A Holiday Snow Angel' in Region S106[1]

[1]Photo courtesy of NASA and STSCi, News Release Number: STScI-2011-38, <hubblesite.org/newscenter>.

Answers from the Bible

1. **Psalms 90:2:** "Before the mountains were brought forth, or ever You had formed the earth and the world, even from everlasting to everlasting, You are God."

   Isaiah 40:28: "Have you not known? Have you not heard? The everlasting God, the LORD, The Creator of the ends of the earth, neither faints nor is weary. His understanding is unsearchable."

   Jeremiah 32:27: "Behold, I am the LORD, the God of all flesh. Is there anything too hard for Me?"

   Daniel 4:35: "All the inhabitants of the earth are reputed as nothing; He does according to His will in the army of heaven and among the inhabitants of the earth. No one can restrain His hand or say to Him, 'What have You done?'"

   Matthew 19:26: "But Jesus looked at them and said to them, 'With men this is impossible, but with God all things are possible.'"

   Revelation 21:6: "And He said to me, 'It is done! I am the Alpha and the Omega, the Beginning and the End. I will give of the fountain of the water of life freely to him who thirsts.'"

2. **Deuteronomy 7:9:** "Therefore know that the LORD your God, He is God, the faithful God who keeps covenant and mercy for a thousand generations with those who love Him and keep His commandments;"

   Jeremiah 23:23-24: "Am I a God near at hand," says the LORD, "And not a God afar off? [24]Can anyone hide himself in secret places, so I shall not see him?" says the LORD; "Do I not fill heaven and earth?" says the LORD.

   Psalm 103 gives praise for God's loving kindness and tender mercies as He remembers that we are but dust.

3. **Numbers 23:19:** "God is not a man, that He should lie, nor a son of man, that He should repent. Has He said, and will He not do? Or has He spoken, and will He not make it good."

4. **Exodus 20:7:** "You shall not take the name of the LORD your God in vain, for the LORD will not hold him guiltless who takes his name in vain."

5.2 God's Holy Nature

No amount of words can describe the triune God of the Bible. As discussed before, the exquisite beauty and specific design of vibrant flowers and butterflies, soaring birds and majestic sequoia trees all point to God's intelligence and love for beauty. Even the weirdest worm, insect or fish testifies to His intention and intricate engineering. The arrangement of the whole universe echoes God's nature. Dr. Henry Morris explained that the universe consists of space, time and matter. These are three distinct entities, but one universe. Similarly, God the Father, Son and Holy Spirit are three persons, but one God.[1]

When God met Moses at the burning bush, He revealed Himself as יהוה. These Hebrew letters "Yod Heh Vav Heh" were later written in Roman scripts as "YHWH," and in English translations as LORD (all capital letters). This name is best translated as "I AM Who I AM" (Exodus 3:14-15). Because the Jews were afraid to blaspheme God's name, they refrained from saying it. Consequently, the true pronunciation of God's holy name was lost. Many pronounce the name as "YAH-way," but more important is the meaning. The LORD God, Yahweh, The Great I AM has no beginning or end. He is an absolute reality, utterly independent and always the same. God has many names describing His different characteristics. For example, El Roi, means "God who sees me," El Shaddai, means "God Almighty" and El Olam means "God Everlasting."

God also introduced Himself as "the Father." Those with an absent or abusive earthly father may find it difficult to relate to this attribute of God. Yet, we all crave a father's acceptance, praise, love and protection. Jesus told us to look at the birds who neither sow nor reap, yet our heavenly Father feeds them, and then asked if we are not of more value than the birds (Matthew 6:26). The apostle John, who loved God dearly, understood the magnitude of the idea that The Great I Am actually yearns to be our Father. He wrote, "Behold what manner of love the Father has bestowed on us, that we should be called children of God!" (1 John 3:1) With infinite wisdom and love, the Heavenly Father wrote a letter (the Bible) to His children through the hands of His servants; a letter of instruction, love, admonition and a revelation of who He is. These words, precious to those who love our heavenly Father, also speak of our heavenly Brother, Christ Jesus.

Every page of the Bible points to Christ Jesus ("Jeshua" in Hebrew). He is the focal point of time. His birth and life divides the world's calendar into a period before (called B.C. - Before Christ, or B.C. E. - Before the Common Era) and after (called A.D. - *anno domini,* "the year of our Lord," or C.E. - Common Era).

---

[1] H. M. Morris, *The beginning of the world, a scientific study of Genesis 1-11.* Master Books. 1977, 19.

Jesus is God the Son and also the image of God the Father. Jesus unmistakably claimed to be God the Son in words (Mark 14:60-65, John 8:58, John 14:7) and action. He forgave sins (Mathew 9:1-8), and gave new laws (Matthew 5, Matthew 22:36-40), something only God can do. The apostle Paul, who met Jesus up-close and personal, described the power and glory of Christ Jesus as follows:

> He is the image of the invisible God, the firstborn of all creation. For by Him all things were created, both in the heavens and on earth, visible and invisible, whether thrones or dominions or rulers or authorities—all things have been created through Him and for Him. He is before all things, and in Him all things hold together. He is also head of the body, the church; and He is the beginning, the firstborn from the dead, so that He Himself will come to have first place in everything. (Colossians 1:15-18)

The Bible clearly establishes the supremacy of Christ Jesus. His majesty is so overwhelming that when Paul and John saw Jesus after His resurrection, they could not remain standing.[1] The almighty King of the universe came to earth for a pre-determined purpose.

Paul continued, "For it was the Father's good pleasure for all the fullness to dwell in Him, and through Him to reconcile all things to Himself, having made peace through the blood of His cross; through Him, I say, whether things on earth or things in heaven." (Colossians 1:19-29) Little did the Roman soldiers know that the crown of thorns they pressed on Jesus' head before nailing Him to the cross, represented the sin of the world.[2] Jesus willfully paid the death penalty for all sin, and nailed our debt to the cross.[3] Death's victory was short-lived though, as Jesus conquered death and rose again on the third day. Therefore, He earned the titles "Lamb of God," "Bread of Life" and "Lord of lords and King of kings!"[4] The prophet Isaiah wrote long before Jesus was born, "For unto us a Child is born, unto us a Son is given; and the government will be upon His shoulder. And His name will be called Wonderful, Counselor, Mighty God, Everlasting Father, Prince of Peace." (Isaiah 9:6)

Today, Jesus is our intercessor, who sits at the right hand of God. On that final day, when He comes to judge the world, He will take all who belong to him to His Father's house. Before He left (about 2,000 years ago), Jesus assured those who believe in Him that His Father's house has many mansions, and that He will prepare a place for them (John 14:1-3). Soon after Jesus' departure, God sent the Holy Spirit in His place.

From all the gifts God gave to mankind, there is none greater than the Holy Spirit. He connects with man's soul to wake him up to his own sin and desperate

---

[1] Acts 9, Revelation 1:17

[2] Thorns are symbolic of sin. Read Genesis 3:17-19, Matthew 13:3-8, Matthew 27:29.

[3] Colossians 2:14-15

[4] John 1:29, John 6:35, Revelation 17:14

situation. He gladly enters the void in the inner chamber to fill it with His blazing light and to guide man with truth.[1] He then testifies that we belong for eternity to the great I AM. Paul wrote, "The Spirit Himself bears witness with our spirit that we are children of God." (Romans 8:16) The Holy Spirit gives believers spiritual gifts to strengthen them and to help them bring glory to God.[2] He is the One who produces fruit of "love, joy, peace, patience, kindness, goodness, faithfulness, gentleness, self-control." (Galatians 5:22) He empowers us to love God and grow in our relationship with Him.

Even though God the Father, Son and Holy Spirit are three distinct persons, they are one God. Our words, ideas and thoughts can barely grasp a glimmer of His holy righteousness, His pure perfection, His infinite greatness and inexhaustible love that cradle the entire universe. How utterly overwhelming is the living triune God, the great I AM.

"The grace of the Lord Jesus Christ, and the love of God, and the communion of the Holy Spirit be with you all. Amen." (2 Corinthians 13:14)

Your Turn to Dig Deeper: God's Holy Nature

1. The words "triune" or "trinity" (three people, but one God) is not in the Bible. How do we know this is God's nature?
    a. How does God refer to Himself in Genesis 1:26 and Genesis 11:7? This may indicate His triune nature or His greatness.
    b. What does God clearly claim in Deuteronomy 6:4?
    c. How does He reveal himself in the New Testament? (Read Matthew 28:19 and 1 John 5:7).
    d. How did Jesus command his followers to baptize others? (Read Matthew 28:19).
    e. Some claim that God just changes from being the Father to the Son to the Holy Spirit. What happened at the river in Matthew 3:16-17?

2. Some think that God was distant in the Old Testament, and only came into a "father-son" relationship after Jesus came to Earth. Is that true? (Read 1 Chronicles 29:10, Proverbs 3:12 and Isaiah 64:8).

3. Even today, many deny that Jesus is God. Some say that only the gospel of John (and none of the others) claims Jesus' deity. (Read John 1:1-4, 14 and John 8:58). They argue that John's gospel was written much later, and by that time, people falsely worshiped Jesus as God.

---

[1] John 16:13

[2] 1 Corinthians 12

a. The gospel of John emphasizes Jesus' deity and spirituality rather than historical issues. However, John did it for a reason. (Read John 20:31).
b. Is John really the only one claiming the deity of Christ? (Read Isaiah 9:6, Mark 14:60-62, 1 Corinthians 12:3, 1 Timothy 3:16, and Hebrews 1:3).

4. After Jesus returned to heaven, the Holy Spirit made a remarkable entrance into the physical world. (Read Acts 2:1-13).
   a. How did He appear, what did He do and how did the people respond?
   b. Put yourself in the listeners' shoes. What would you have thought?

Answers from the Bible

1a. **Genesis 1:26:** "Then God said, 'Let Us make man in Our image, according to Our likeness ..."

Genesis 11:7: "Come, let Us go down and there confuse their language, that they may not understand one another's speech."

1b. **Deuteronomy 6:4:** "Hear, O Israel: The LORD our God, the LORD is one!"

1c. **Matthew 28:19:** "Go therefore and make disciples of all the nations, baptizing them in the name of the Father and of the Son and of the Holy Spirit."

1 John 5:7: "For there are three that bear witness in heaven: the Father, the Word, and the Holy Spirit; and these three are one."

1d. **Matthew 28:19:** "Go therefore and make disciples of all the nations, baptizing them in the name of the Father and of the Son and of the Holy Spirit."

1e. **Matthew 3:16-17:** "When He had been baptized, Jesus came up immediately from the water; and behold, the heavens were opened to Him, and He saw the Spirit of God descending like a dove and alighting upon Him. 17And suddenly a voice came from heaven, saying, 'This is My beloved Son, in whom I am well pleased.'"

2. **1 Chronicles 29:10:** "Therefore David blessed the LORD before all the assembly; and David said: 'Blessed are You, LORD God of Israel, our Father, forever and ever.'"

   Proverbs 3:12: "For whom the LORD loves He corrects, just as a father the son in whom he delights."

   Isaiah 64:8: "But now, O LORD, You are our Father; We are the clay, and You our potter; And all we are the work of Your hand."

3. **John 1:1-4, 14:** "In the beginning was the Word, and the Word was with God, and the Word was God. 2He was in the beginning with God. 3All things were made through Him, and without Him nothing was made that was made. 4In Him was life, and the life was the light of men. 14And the Word became flesh and dwelt among us, and we beheld His glory, the glory as of the only begotten of the Father, full of grace and truth."

John 8:58: "Jesus said to them, 'Most assuredly, I say to you, before Abraham was, I AM.'"

3a. **John 20:31:** " ... but these are written that you may believe that Jesus is the Christ, the Son of God, and that believing you may have life in His name."

3b. **Isaiah 9:6:** "For unto us a Child is born, unto us a Son is given; And the government will be upon His shoulder. And His name will be called Wonderful, Counselor, Mighty God, Everlasting Father, Prince of Peace."

Mark 14:60-62: (NASB) "The high priest stood up and came forward and questioned Jesus, saying, "Do You not answer? What is it that these men are testifying against You?" [61] But He kept silent and did not answer. Again the high priest was questioning Him, and saying to Him, "Are You the Christ, the Son of the Blessed One?" [62] And Jesus said, "I am; and you shall see the Son of Man sitting at the right hand of Power, and coming with the clouds of heaven."

1 Corinthians 12:3: "Therefore I make known to you that no one speaking by the Spirit of God calls Jesus accursed, and no one can say that Jesus is Lord except by the Holy Spirit."

1 Timothy 3:16: "And without controversy great is the mystery of godliness: God was manifested in the flesh, justified in the Spirit, seen by angels, preached among the Gentiles, believed on in the world, received up in glory."

Hebrews 1:3: "... who being the brightness of His glory and the express image of His person, and upholding all things by the word of His power, when He had by Himself purged our sins, sat down at the right hand of the Majesty on high."

4. **Acts 2:1-13:** (NASB) "When the day of Pentecost had come, they were all together in one place. [2] And suddenly there came from heaven a noise like a violent rushing wind, and it filled the whole house where they were sitting. [3] And there appeared to them tongues as of fire distributing themselves, and they rested on each one of them. [4] And they were all filled with the Holy Spirit and began to speak with other tongues, as the Spirit was giving them utterance.[5] Now there were Jews living in Jerusalem, devout men from every nation under heaven. [6] And when this sound occurred, the crowd came together, and were bewildered because each one of them was hearing them speak in his own language. [7] They were amazed and astonished, saying, 'Why, are not all these who are speaking Galileans? [8] And how is it that we each hear them in our own language to which we were born? [9] Parthians and Medes and Elamites, and residents of Mesopotamia, Judea and Cappadocia, Pontus and Asia, [10] Phrygia and Pamphylia, Egypt and the districts of Libya around Cyrene, and visitors from Rome, both Jews and proselytes, [11] Cretans and Arabs—we hear them in our own tongues speaking of the mighty deeds of God.' [12] And they all continued in amazement and great perplexity, saying to one another, 'What does this mean?' [13] But others were mocking and saying, 'They are full of sweet wine.'"

5.3 God's Perfect Love

The all-important puzzle piece of love must fit in the right place in the puzzle. But where? Science cannot explain it, man dreams about it and the Bible tells about it. God, however, IS love. He is the author of love, and the only one whose love is perfect. Some find it hard to believe.

When Adam and Eve ate the forbidden fruit in the garden, their human eyes were opened, but their eyes to see God were blinded. They lost their intimate love relationship with God. On top of that, God banned them from the beautiful Garden of Eden, destined to a life of backbreaking labor, pain and suffering. A bit severe for just taking a bite, some say. A pastor once explained it as follows. He asked people to fill in the blank: God was so _____ that he chased Adam and Eve out of the Garden of Eden. You see, the word you choose reflects your view of God. Is it "angry," "intolerant" or "unfair?" Perhaps you have an abusive father, so unreasonable treatment is exactly what you expect from God. Especially since He is our heavenly Father.

After His talk with Adam and Eve hiding in the bushes, the LORD God said, "Behold, the man has become like one of Us, to know good and evil. And now, lest he put out his hand and take also of the tree of life, and eat, and live forever –" (Genesis 3:22) Stop a moment to think why God didn't want them to live forever. The answer may blow your mind. Man's relationship with God was broken. If man lived forever in his fleshly body, then the broken state would be irreversible. Only death can set us free from this sin-stained body, so we can share the same intimate relationship with God that Adam and Eve enjoyed prior to their disobedience. The answer, therefore, in the blank space should be "loving." God was so loving that he chased Adam and Eve out of the Garden of Eden. It is almost like a parent shoving his child off the road to save his life.

God showed His love and mercy not only to Adam and Eve, but also to people and nations throughout history. The Bible is filled with people who experienced His amazing love such as Enoch, Abraham, Moses, Daniel, David, Elijah, Ruth, Stephen, John and Paul to name a few. He made His ultimate stand at the cross. Paul wrote, "But God demonstrates His own love toward us, in that while we were still sinners, Christ died for us." (Romans 5:8) To Timothy he wrote, "For this is good and acceptable in the sight of God our Savior, who desires all men to be saved and to come to the knowledge of the truth. For there is one God and one Mediator between God and men, the Man Christ Jesus, who gave Himself a ransom for all, to be testified in due time." (1 Timothy 2:3-6) Little people could not crucify the King of the universe; He let them do it while extending His forgiveness to them. They could not take His life; He willingly laid it down because He loved us first.

God is also the author of intimacy. Today, most connect this word with physical intimacy. However, physical intimacy is nothing without spiritual intimacy. Intimacy is about mutual trust, respect, loyalty and the deep joy of companionship. God instituted the marriage between a man and a woman, not only for procreation, but also for intimacy. Unlike popular opinion that marriage is all about your own "happily ever after," the true meaning of an earthly marriage is for us to grow in our intimacy with God.

Through the joys and trials of our marital relationships, we learn about loyalty, self-denial, trust, commitment and spiritual intimacy. We mostly learn through mistakes and get plenty of opportunities to practice forgiveness and grace. This gives us a glimpse of how much God loves us, and what it takes to live our lives set apart for Him. The Bible describes God's people as the bride and Jesus as the bridegroom.[1] The reason being that when a husband and wife become one the way God intended, it is a picture of the ultimate loyalty and spiritual intimacy that God himself desires from His children.

How inconceivable is His great love for us, how staggering the fact that the King of the universe wants us to know Him personally. He asks you to love Him with all your heart, all your soul and all your mind (Matthew 22:37). And who better to give yourself to? No earthly friend can compare with His perfect love, His awareness of your deepest needs and His unfailing protection and guidance. In the midst of suffering and unanswered questions, you are safe with Him for eternity.

"So that Christ may dwell in your hearts through faith; and that you, being rooted and grounded in love, may be able to comprehend with all the saints what is the breadth and length and height and depth, and to know the love of Christ which surpasses knowledge, that you may be filled up to all the fullness of God." (Ephesians 3:17-19, NASB)

Your turn to dig deeper: God's Perfect Love

1. What is love? (Romans 5:8, 1 Corinthians 13:4-8, 1 John 3:18 and 1 John 4:8).
2. I find Paul's definition of love in 1 Corinthians 13:4-7 extremely challenging. Are you mad or bitter at someone close to you? How have you justified your thoughts and actions? Read these verses again and use them as a measuring stick to evaluate your love.
3. In what ways does God describe the relationship He wants with man? (Read Matthew 6:9 and Matthew 7:9-11).
    a. What is your relationship with your father? How does it influence your relationship with your Heavenly Father?

[1] Matthew 5:1-13, Revelation 21:9

   b. What symbolizes the relationship between Christ Jesus and man? (Read Revelation 19:7-9).
   c. Can you agree that God desires a personal relationship with man?

4. What does God require from you? (Read Deuteronomy 6:5, Micah 6:8 and John 14:15).

Answers from the Bible

1. **Romans 5:8:** "But God demonstrates His own love toward us, in that while we were still sinners, Christ died for us."
   1 Corinthians 13:4-7: (NASB) "Love is patient, love is kind and is not jealous; love does not brag and is not arrogant, [5] does not act unbecomingly; it does not seek its own, is not provoked, does not take into account a wrong suffered, [6]does not rejoice in unrighteousness, but rejoices with the truth;[7] bears all things, believes all things, hopes all things, endures all things."
   1 John 3:18: "My little children, let us not love in word or in tongue, but in deed and in truth."
   1 John 4:8: "He who does not love does not know God, for God is love."

3. **Matthew 6:9:** "In this manner, therefore, pray: Our Father in heaven, Hallowed be Your name."
   Matthew 7:9-11: "Or what man is there among you who, if his son asks for bread, will give him a stone? [10]Or if he asks for a fish, will he give him a serpent? [11]If you then, being evil, know how to give good gifts to your children, how much more will your Father who is in heaven give good things to those who ask Him!"

3b. **Revelation 19:7-9:** "Let us be glad and rejoice and give Him glory, for the marriage of the Lamb has come, and His wife has made herself ready. [8]And to her it was granted to be arrayed in fine linen, clean and bright, for the fine linen is the righteous acts of the saints. [9]Then he said to me, 'Write: Blessed are those who are called to the marriage supper of the Lamb!' And he said to me, 'These are the true sayings of God.'"

4. **Deuteronomy 6:5:** "You shall love the LORD your God with all your heart, with all your soul, and with all your strength."
   Micah 6:8: "He has shown you, O man, what good; and what does the LORD require of you but to do justly, to love mercy, and to walk humbly with your God?"
   John 14:15: "If you love me, keep my commandments."

Chapter 6

The Reason to Believe

"On a Friday, just outside Jerusalem, Roman soldiers erected a cross on the crest of the hill Golgoth, 'Skull Hill.' Nobody had any idea at the time that it marked a major intersection between heaven and hell. But between the hours of twelve and three on a Friday, it was the site of a cosmic crash, the effects of which has continued to reverberate for two thousand years throughout the world."[1] They buried His broken body in a tomb. But three days later, when Christ Jesus rose from the dead and left the tomb empty, He became the ultimate reason to believe!

The message of this last chapter is simple. God intended it for a child to understand. Yet, it carries the weight of life and death. If you had 10 minutes to live, this will be all that matters regardless of your wealth, status, age or accomplishments.

Above is the drawing of page three, the Life Puzzle with the four corners of God, science, truth, and man. This time, a cross, the symbol of forgiveness, guards

[1] E. H. Peterson, *Tell it Slant.* Wm, B. Eerdmans Publishing Company, 2008, 250.

the gate. Notice that the hiker's road dead ends at terrifying cliffs. The only turnoff point is at a gate. Only a hiker pure, spotless and without any fault, is free to enter through the gate and follow the road up the mountain instead. Unfortunately, he cannot physically see beyond the end of either roads untill he arrives, and by then there is no turning back.

The hiker's roads are our roads. By default, we all travel on the road that ends at the cliffs, because we all have sinned and fall short of the glory of God.[1] If we do nothing, our lives will end in eternal separation from God in a place called hell. Hell is a place God originally prepared for Satan and his followers.[2] Since it is void of God's presence, only darkness, intense loneliness, fear, desperation, guilt and dreadful anguish awaits all who go there. There is just one alternative.

Turn off at the cross and enter through the gate. Jesus said, "I am the way, the truth, and the life. No one comes to the Father except through Me." The moment you pass through that gate, you are washed white as snow.[3] You gain a loving Father, the most brilliant and royal big Brother and the sweet Holy Spirit to guide and comfort you on your life's journey to your heavenly home. The choice seems easy. Why, then, do so few make it?

Perhaps, because they can't see beyond the end of their road, they ignore the existence of the spiritual realm. Perhaps, because no one warned them. Maybe they are having too much fun right now, or are too busy serving the master of this world. Some blame the hypocrisy of self-proclaimed Christians. When asked why she returned to her Buddhist faith, a lady once said, "Look at the Christians!" Sad, but often true. Only Christ is perfect. However, do not be deceived. Not all who claim to be Christians are real. Jesus warned, "Not everyone who says to Me, 'Lord, Lord,' shall enter the kingdom of heaven, but he who does the will of My Father in heaven. Many will say to Me in that day, 'Lord, Lord, have we not prophesied in Your name, cast out demons in Your name, and done many wonders in Your name?' And then I will declare to them, 'I never knew you; depart from Me, you who practice lawlessness!'"(Matthew 7:21-23)

The list of excuses to refuse God's greatest gift is long, but perhaps the root issue is twofold: No reason to believe and refusal to surrender control. You see, making this choice is all about believe and surrender. You can be a brilliant scholar with many titles knowing much about God, man and science galore. Yet, until you believe that Jesus died on the cross to pay the penalty for your sin, accept His forgiveness after admission of your guilt, and submit to Him as King and Ruler of your life, you have missed the gate. Jesus said, "For God so loved the world that He

[1] Romans 3:23

[2] Matthew 25:41

[3] Isaiah 1:18

gave His only begotten Son, that whoever believes in Him, should not perish but have eternal life." (John 3:16)

Choosing to go through the gate is not a good deed, it is merely the acceptance of the greatest gift. You cannot afford the entrance fee anyway, since the penalty for sin is death. Your best efforts contribute absolutely nothing towards the ticket price. Paul wrote, "For by grace you have been saved through faith, and that not of yourselves; it is the gift of God, not of works, lest anyone should boast." (Ephesians 2:8-9) The entrance is totally free, but it comes with a requirement.

Jesus said, "If anyone desires to come after Me, let him deny himself, and take up his cross, and follow Me." (Matthew 16:24) You must deny yourself, because God's kingdom is not a democracy, and it is not a place for corrupt human ideas. You must take up your cross, because your body is still corrupt and will make war against the idea of giving up some dirty worldly pleasures and desires. Satan, who "prowls around like a lion," (1Peter 5:8) will be sure to remind you of those, since he never quits trying to destroy you. You must put on the "whole armor of God" to be able to withstand Satan and his wicked companions (Ephesians 6:10-18). You must follow Jesus, because His Word is the only lamp to your feet and light to your path[1] to guide you safely up the mountain. When you fully comprehend the extent of His love, protection and guidance, you gladly follow with a heart overflowing with gratitude.

Jesus does not ask you to do the impossible though. He enables you. Upon your invitation, the Holy Spirit enters your inner chamber; He lights up the place and does an extreme makeover. Paul wrote, "Therefore, if anyone is in Christ, he is a new creation; old things have passed away; behold, all things have become new." (2 Corinthians 5:17) Paul also asks, "Or do you not know that your body is the temple of the Holy Spirit who is in you, whom you have from God, and you are not your own? For you were bought at a price." (1 Corinthians 6:19-20)

Once you pass through the gate, you need to find true believers to share the journey up the mountain. God did not intend for you to walk by yourself. As a coal needs to be in the fire to glow, so believers need fellowship, encouragement and accountability to grow spiritually. You can rest in Jesus' promise that no one will ever snatch you out of His hand, and nothing will separate you from His love.[2] Just keep your eyes on Jesus, it is so easy to forget His way when the storms come. God never said that the road up the mountain would be easy, but rather that He will be with you every step of the way. Consult your Bible daily; it is your priceless map for this road. Be sensitive to the guidance of the Holy Spirit. He will not shout above your noisy busyness. You will hear Him when you are quiet before the LORD. Your goal is to reach the top of the mountain and say, like Paul, "I have fought the good fight, I have finished the race, I have kept the faith." (2 Timothy 4:7)

---

[1] Psalm 119:105

[2] John 10:28, Romans 8:35-39

Why waste another day enjoying fake pleasures, when real joy is one choice away. After adding so many pieces to your puzzle, it may be clear that science cannot explain everything, that the Bible is the only reliable source of truth, that God loves you and you are lost without Him. This is not blind faith, you have all the reasons to believe, and God is calling you right now. Do not pass the gate, you may not have time to turn back.

Tell God about the things in your life that you know will wither in His spotlight of righteousness. Accept that Jesus paid your debt in full, and ask His forgiveness. He is faithful to forgive and completely clean the truly repentant heart. Surrender your heart, mind and soul to your heavenly King and Master. God promised many times in the Bible that if you do this, you will enter through the gate and become His child. Some of these promises are listed below. Find one and make it your own. Write it down on paper, on your heart, and in your mind. It is your sword against Satan and his lies. You are now a child of the living God and on the road to your real home!

"But as many as received Him, to them He gave the right to become children of God, to those who believe in His name." (John 1:12)

"Most assuredly, I say to you, he who hears My word and believes in Him who sent Me has everlasting life, and shall not come into judgment, but has passed from death into life." (John 5:24)

"And this is the will of Him who sent Me, that everyone who sees the Son and believes in Him may have everlasting life; and I will raise him up at the last day." (John 6:40)

"And it shall come to pass that whoever calls on the name of the Lord shall be saved." (Acts 2:21)

"That if you confess with your mouth the Lord Jesus and believe in your heart that God has raised Him from the dead, you will be saved." (Romans 10:9)

"Therefore He is also able to save to the uttermost those who come to God through Him, since He always lives to make intercession for them." (Hebrews 7:25)

"Now to Him who is able to keep you from stumbling, and to present you faultless before the presence of His glory with exceeding joy, to God our Savior, who alone is wise, be glory and majesty, dominion and power, both now and forever. Amen." (Jude 24 and 25)

Author's Note

I have already trekked quite a distance up the mountain. The view up here is striking. I gaze down on a bigger picture, with more perspective and clarity; a picture that was invisible when I started at the foothills so many years ago. I notice many puzzle pieces are still missing, and that is okay. I know I'll find them all, eventually, once I get to heaven.

I arrived here, not on my own steam, nor my own wisdom. In fact, I regret the times I stubbornly took control only to find myself tangled in detours, hurts, self-pity and missed opportunities. I am often overwhelmed by my King's patience, mercy, and unmerited favor. He did not give me what I sometimes foolishly asked for. He often provided before I could ask, in ways I could not have imagined. During the darkest and most desperate times, I could be quiet knowing He is God.

The journey, so far, has been quite a ride with countless miracles, twists and turns. Along the way, I met sweet friends who shared their amazing stories. In fact, everyone traveling up the mountain has stories to share. Some are unbearably sad, others exciting, but they are always beautiful when we look back. The most thrilling part of the story is that we are on our way to our real home. Every day is a day closer to the moment will we be in God's presence, immersed in His boundless love and surrounded by His breathtaking glory!

Acknowledgements

Dad, you led me to God, taught me His Word daily, and showed me the way through your own faithful and joyful journey. Thank you for patiently reading many drafts, for your valuable advice and for the much needed cheering. To my husband, Marius, thank you for your encouragement and insight. For almost 30 years, you have been an inspiration to reach for excellence and go the extra mile. A big thanks to my three sons. It was fun sharing the book writing process with you! Your straight shooting kept me on track. My sis Reen, thank you for your support and endless hours making little puzzle pieces. Christine thanks for editing and Steve, for a beautiful book cover that says a thousand words. My deepest gratitude is towards my King, who took me on this amazing journey. He showered me with His grace, mercy, goodness and love along the way. This book is worth nothing unless it glorifies You.

www.ingramcontent.com/pod-product-compliance
Ingram Content Group UK Ltd.
Pitfield, Milton Keynes, MK11 3LW, UK
UKHW061306190726
13851UKWH00020B/139